THE SON OF CRISIS

The business history of Marco Stefanini,
Founder of
Stefanini IT Solutions

By
Rogério Godinho

Title: The Son of Crisis
Author: Rogério Godinho

ISBN: 978-1-7394329-5-9

Published by Woodbridge Publishers
1280 Lexington Ave STE 2
New York, NY 10028

Printed in United States of America

WOODBRIDGE
PUBLISHERS

TABLE OF CONTENTS

ACKNOWLEDGMENTS

THE MERIT IS THEIRS

The concept of authorship is riddled with imprecision. Like most others, this book would not exist without the help of countless individuals. It is to them that I attribute the merits of what is right about it while exempting them from any demerits in the work, which are evidently my own doing.

First, without any demagoguery, I would like to profoundly thank the businessman Marco Stefanini. In addition to having a very worthy history, he is the dream subject for any biographer. He clarified moments of uncertainty and unrestrictedly accepted everything that my investigations uncovered. I am pleased to say that no part of this story was censured and that it is arriving at the reader like it was discovered: complete and unbiased.

I acknowledge my debt of gratitude to all characters who experienced the stories in this book and who were so generous in entrusting me with their memories.

Equally indispensable were those who, while not appearing in these pages, helped me obtain crucial information for the interest and due progression of the story or who somehow granted me valuable insights throughout the development of the book. These people are: Argemiro Leite, Débora Freire, Edemar Antonio Wolf de Paula, Germana Anghinoni, Gilberto Andrade, Juliana Perri, Lúcia Porto, Marcelo Montenegro, Marici Gomes Góes, Nadja Costa, Nilton Cruz, Oscar Siqueira, Alexandre Mendes Freitas, Roberta Salles, Rômulo Soares, Sandra Becker, Wesley Mamprim and Yuri Oliveira. For the second edition, a specific executive was essential: Carla Alessandra de Figueiredo

iv

Silva, who brought contacts, information, and stories, always with a clever and sensible perspective.

After the investigation, a valuable group came into play. These people made supremely precious contributions, indicating errors, imperfections, and mistakes. This was the priceless work of Isamu Suzuki, Júlio Wiziack, Patrícia Rúbia do Nascimento, Maria Teresa do Nascimento, Vinicius Pinheiro, and Thiago Borges. They made this book that much better.

Last, and definitely not least, I must thank the support offered by my soul mate, Érika Suzuki. From the investigation of facts to the writing of the initial draft, up until the last details of the text, she has truly been my co-author. Without her, there would truly be no book to speak of, for the results would have amounted to a pile of text unworthy of publication. To her, I extend all of my love.

And to all other individuals mentioned, my eternal gratitude.

Rogério Godinho

PREFACE

At times, life can feel like it's made up of one crisis after another. Whether those crises are personal or professional, local or global, learning how to take calculated steps forward when others are stopping in their tracks is one of the keys to success – especially for an entrepreneur.

Marco Stefanini is no stranger to adversity, facing market destabilization, inflation, and other economic barriers early in his career. But entrepreneurs often face uncertainty, and Marco would encounter crises many times on his journey from a young man building his company from the ground up to the Founder and Global CEO of that same company, which now operates in more than 41 countries around the world.

Marco's company, Stefanini Group, has seen its fair share of crisis as well – most recently in the form of the COVID-19 pandemic, which halted business operations for many companies around the world. But while other companies were struggling to determine how to maintain business as usual, Stefanini Group continued to be guided by Marco's entrepreneurial spirit, looking for ways to capitalize on crisis. This led to one of the most transformative periods in the company's history, with Stefanini Group acquiring more than 14 companies from the beginning of the pandemic to date, reaffirming its ability to meet current demand and organize for the future.

Bringing new companies into the fold increased Stefanini Group's ability to deliver results, but to incorporate new ventures and capabilities into the group without muddling the brand identity, maintaining one brand architecture became more important than ever before. Following decades of growth and reinvention, Stefanini Group is one company composed of many, but the brand remains rooted in the principles of entrepreneurship and the mission of co-creating solutions for a better future.

On this path to a better future, the company is bound to face new challenges, but with a lien architecture, agile work process, and human approach, Stefanini Group has prepared itself to stand the test of time. The adaptability and resilience of Marco's company is a reflection of the man himself, visualized through the chapters of this story. Successfully navigating crises is the mark of a true entrepreneur and this book proves that Marco Stefanini's entrepreneurial spirit is alive and well across his organization.

Sir Martin Sorrell,
Founder & Executive Chairman of S4 Capital
and Founder of WPP

PROLOGUE

Graça Sajovic turned on the TV at the hotel and saw a surreal landscape. The news program was showing the dazzling Italian city of Milan.

"Marco, you have to see this," she said, calling up her husband.

Rather than a newscast, it looked like a scene out of a disaster movie. A day before that, on Wednesday, March 11, 2020, the Italian Prime Minister had suspended all commercial activities in the country, with the exception of supermarkets and drugstores. Official estimates pointed to 15,000 cases and over a thousand deaths in Italian territory by that moment. As a result, the country shut down: deserted streets, closed parks, stores with locked doors, and children stuck at home.

The couple wasn't in São Paulo, where they lived, but nearly eight thousand kilometers away, in Mexico City. Marco Stefanini, founder of the company that carried his name, and Graça, his wife and the company's vice-president, had just arrived to visit their Mexican branch, with plans to later extend their trip to the United States. Although unreal scenes were shocking the entire world by that point, few could imagine the events that were about to unfold.

SARS-CoV-2, the virus responsible for Covid-19, was turning the world into a science-fiction scenario. Causing over six million deaths, it would force people to stay at home, reducing economic activity to unprecedented levels in modern history.

From the business perspective, this was the highest impact since the Great Depression in 1929, which had the Dow Jones index fall by 66% in a little over two months. This time around, a microscopic threat immobilized the world and shrunk the financial indicator by 38.4% in less than six weeks. The stock market anticipated events to come in real economy. The scenes seen by the Stefanini couple on TV would soon come to pass – fully or partially – in all countries. For the first time in the history of civilization, a single event would affect every corner of the planet, from Beijing to the Amazon, from Paris to the Argentinean Tierra del Fuego, from New York to small islands in the Pacific Ocean.

Entrepreneurs were left to face the threat in the economic realm. In Europe, industry was the sector that suffered the most. In the Stefanini portfolio alone, around 300 clients were shutting down their factories, no longer requiring the company's services – for a while, at least. Throughout the world, acquisition plans were suspended, investments interrupted, and hiring processes frozen. Mass layoffs were almost certain to occur.

Crises wouldn't easily startle Stefanini. Marco had established the company in a country known for its instability, whether due to the inflation, international influences, or changes in the business environment. This time around, however, the adverse scenario was affecting a globalized Stefanini. It competed with giants in Asia and Europe, in the United States and in Latin America. It had faced the hardships in integrating multiple culture, carrying and consolidating its DNA in the over 40 countries where it was active. All of this while carrying out acquisitions and adding value to services in a market that changed at breakneck speeds.

It was at this unique moment in Stefanini's history that Marco and Graça were far from home, precisely in the week that countries began to close their borders and flights were canceled. That's when one of the most internationally-driven companies in Brazil was to face its most demanding trial, the definitive test for the culture and identity they so valued, watching the transformation around them. When Stefanini, known for thriving in the direst of moments, would face its largest crisis of all. After that, everything would be different.

CHAPTER 1

DISARRAY

The rain drenched the pale green bush. Here and there, if one paid attention, it'd be possible to find some blue (the wolf's plant blossom) or yellow (pequi). Young Marco Stefanini, however, could not help but watch the pouring rain and wonder what a man from São Paulo was doing in the middle of the Goiás' cerrado, over 1,500 kilometers from home.

It was February 1984, and Brazil was undergoing its most intense economic crisis in 150 years of capitalism. Unemployment was a blight on 8.96% of the population, the worst level in the following 25 years. The inflation the year prior reached 211%. Uncertainty abounded, and the people were on the streets clamoring for direct elections. Marco, aged 23, graduated in Geology since the end of 1983, was at the crossroads faced by unemployed youth.

If he looked to his side, it got even worse. His sister, Mônica, four years his junior, was in the second year of college and working an internship job. His girlfriend, Graça, had graduated in Psychology and was working as an intern at the youth detention center Febem. Marco, a graduate of the University of São Paulo (USP), couldn't manage to make ends meet.

These circumstances led Marco Stefanini to the pouring cerrado rain, right in the middle of a huge economic crisis.

The boy excelled in exact sciences and humanities, but biology was never one of his strengths. First came the interest in studying history; the shelves at his childhood home always carried biographies of major personalities. His mother, Adélia – an adept reader –, knew that and encouraged him to study History, but the boy wanted something with better professional opportunities and chose Engineering.

In the second year of High School, he second-guessed himself and figured he wouldn't be a good engineer, as he had never cared much for details. Marco enjoyed being challenged, seeking ventures, and learning.

He opened a manual on the USP admission exam, Fuvest, and began to read the section on professions involving exact sciences. That was when he read about Geology. "Would you look at that, Geology is part of the exact sciences," he thought. "Better yet, it's got something to do with Chemistry."

To the area's supreme advantage, geologists are required to travel often, and Marco always enjoyed traveling. He would save every penny made on odd jobs to be able to fund trips with friends. He also wasn't at all interested in wearing a tie or being overly formal, and Geology felt quite informal. In 1978, when he chose his profession, Geology was still held in high regard in Brazil and was one of the most well-paid jobs for beginners.

He did not give up on Engineering that easily, however. While he did apply for Civil Engineering at a few private colleges, he gave up on building bridges and houses when admitted to the Geology program at USP. He was to become a Geologist.

Four years later, the option didn't seem so good in hindsight.

He wondered whether he had attended the wrong course or even the wrong university. Possibilities began to dwindle, and even Petrobras, which always appeared to offer good job opportunities, was suffering from the crisis; 94% of cars made in Brazil were being released with engines running on ethanol. And Petrobras was an oasis in the mining market. Geology now seemed to have been a terrible choice.

At the end of his program, after seeing all his colleagues getting internship opportunities or jobs, his chance finally came. Upon graduating in December, Marco's job came up in January. The business group that employed this young geologist had a newly acquired cassiterite mountain in Goiás (Marco later discovered that almost all of the mining machines were idle because the company had filed for bankruptcy). In any case, the offer appeared to be promising. Cassiterite is the source of tin, and that year, Brazil was about to double its exports of the metal, the only one with which the country had recorded a trade surplus in the previous ten-year period.

However, that adventure in Goiás was about to have an awkward start.

A friend had given his recommendation for the job, and it appeared to Marco that the person hiring him was excessively boastful. He was a manager, rather than the owner; nevertheless, he flew out of Goiânia in a private jet, stayed at a nice hotel and attended fancy restaurants.

In early January 1984, Marco flew in with him and, when arriving in Goiânia, they drove north for a whole day, for over 500 kilometers, to the approximate location where the border with Tocantins currently stands. The northernmost portion was the poorer part of Goiás, usually neglected by the authorities – one of the reasons why Tocantins would become a separate state years later. However, right where Marco stood, a lot of ore had been discovered in recent years in cities such as Minaçu, Nova Roma, and Cavalcante. Cassiterite, in turn, was one of the main treasures coveted by miners.

Ultimately, they stopped the car before a river. They boarded a barge and went up against the water, watching tapirs and capybaras peacefully grazing on the sparse vegetation. For a young man from São Paulo more familiar with streets and

3

buildings, it all felt like a painting, with a surreal tinge to it. After a few hours in the humid heat, the barge stopped.

The manager pointed to a wooden shed amidst the bushes where the office was located. Marco took his affairs and left the barge. He looked back, knowing that if that barge broke down, they would all be helplessly stranded for at least three days.

The cassiterite mine was nowhere to be seen yet. To arrive there, Marco drove for 20 kilometers more on a dirt road, one so poorly kept that no one would take at night. It made more sense to stay at the mine. The wet season in Goiás meant it was pouring rain.

Marco actually slept in a hammock since the mine lacked a minimal tent. Wherever he looked, the young geologist could only see tall bushes and trees with gnarled branches and thick bark.

He stayed there for a week. Finally, he came back to the office shed and was told to take the jet back to São Paulo to run lab tests on the samples collected in Goiás. The jet gave out a good impression, but a dire surprise came when it was time to get paid. The company only offered the Goiás minimum wage, which was different from the amount paid in São Paulo. Marco reacted poorly in his rebellious youth: he sneered, complained, grumbled, kicked and screamed, but ultimately accepted his pay.

There were further disappointments to come. Petrobras was also an oasis in the market because it granted employees more resting time. They would work for fifteen days and take the next fifteen off. Resting is more than necessary – employees stay in remote and completely isolated regions, often in unhealthy circumstances.

In other mining operations – outside the state-owned oasis – it was more common to work for 30 days and then take 15 days off. In simple mathematical terms, that is like working five weekdays and taking Saturday and Sunday off. Considering isolation and other disadvantages, the outlook is not all that positive.

When Marco went to Goiânia, he had an even rawer deal: working 45 days and taking 15 days off. Sure, for a first job, after all that time searching, this wasn't going to sour the deal.

On the same day of the disappointment due to the Goiás minimum wage, his manager called the new employee and warned him: "You have 15 days off but will have to work for 60 days straight." Marco complied.

Even in his rebelliousness, he bowed his head to nearly all the demands, not wanting to give up. He could kick and scream, but his entire professional future seemed to depend on that first job—sleeping in a hammock, staying away from family and friends, from everyone he knew, barely getting paid, and having no time off.

That was when Marco received a one-way ticket to the cassiterite mine. He complained and asked for a return ticket. The manager said he would give him one later. Marco would have been entirely dependent on him, lost in the middle of nowhere and under the pouring rain.

He gave up on the entire deal. The refusal took him out of the Goiás cerrado and brought him back to the São Paulo concrete jungle, where he would look for what to do with his life. The month of March 1984 was just beginning, and Marco was once again in the throes of unemployment.

That crisis had started to worsen two years prior when the geologist was in his third year of college. Mexico asked for a debt moratorium in September 1982, and over 40 countries asked the International Monetary Fund (IMF) for help in its wake. International banks automatically lost trust in Brazil, and foreign currency reserves fell from USD 3 billion to zero within two months. In December, Brazil started paying only interest on the debt, in a sort of disguised moratorium. Two months later, the Cruzeiro currency suffered an overshooting of 30%; four months later, in June 1983, the government indexed wages and imposed a real loss of 30%. The popularity of President João Figueiredo plummeted, and the political crisis spread like wildfire.

It was in the midst of this situation in the Brazilian economy that the young geologist got his degree—perhaps the worst economic crisis in the history of Brazil under capitalism. It was also within an economic crisis that the Stefanini saga began in the country, nearly 80 years prior when José Stefanini, Marco's great-great-grandfather, left Ravenna, in the Center-North portion of Italy (the North is the region where the Stefanini name is believed to have originated, with the oldest record belonging to Antônio Stefanini in the 17th century).

The situation in Ravenna, as in Italy as a whole, was far from good, with a deficit reaching 4% of the federal public budget. It was the third year of an economic crisis that started in 1887.

At that time in Brazil, abolitionist laws threatened to remove slave labor from farms, and Viscount Parnaíba, the governor of the Province of São Paulo, traveled through Europe in search of people willing to escape that crisis by making a living in Brazil. In 1886, farmers from the state of São Paulo took matters into their own hands and founded Sociedade Promotora da Imigração, an association for the promotion of immigration.

When young José Stefanini arrived in Brazil in 1889, one year after the liberation of black slaves, 18,000 Italian families had already settled in Brazil, with over 100,000 oriundi (descendants of Italians born in Brazil). The society created by the farmers preferred families to single workers, and José was exactly the type they were looking for, bringing his wife Júlia Forbueze and

6

their child Francisco, who was 6 years old at the time. The family stayed for a few days at the Inn of the Immigrants, like all the new arrivals from the Italian steamships. They then boarded the São Paulo Railway train.

They got off the train in Rafard, a municipality in the São Paulo state countryside that was part of the Capivari district at the time. Soon, they moved to Salto, around 40 kilometers away and closer to the São Paulo state capital. At the time, the place was called Salto de Itu, named precisely because it was economically dependent on its neighboring municipality, Itu, which had a reputation for producing large objects and coffee, as well as being one of the centers of power in São Paulo. Salto de Itu did not make coffee or large products, but it ended up harboring a textile industry.

Francisco lived a joyful life with a joyful family. A storytelling Italian type, he had a sense of humor and enjoyed drinking with friends. One time, he got on the streetcar coming back from the bar and paid the toll collector. Suddenly, the collector asked him for the fee again. And then a third time.

The fourth time, Francisco lost his cool:

– Enough! Why do I have to pay you again?

– Because you slept on the bench and this is the fourth time you've made the trip already!

However, the story of most consequence for his relatives was when Francisco had a child, whom he wished to register as Duílio, an Italian name. Francisco wanted Duílio, and Duílio it would be. He left home for the registry office with that intention and came back home calling his son Duílio.

Eighteen years later, the boy found out that his name was actually Dovídio Stefanini. The clerk at the registry office thought Duílio was too Italian and preferred to register the boy with a less foreign-sounding name. Francisco came back home without saying a word, and Marco's grandfather bore two different names.

Dovídio (or Duílio) was more austere and serious than his father; he left Salto to fight Getúlio Vargas during the 1932 Revolution. The fight between the federal government and the state of São Paulo is considered to be the greatest Brazilian civil war, and it started right in the middle of the 1929 economic crisis, which drove coffee prices down. Dependent on the bean, the economy of São Paulo suffered, and President Washington Luís (a São Paulo native) broke the agreement established with the state of Minas Gerais in 1899.

Both states were wealthy, but São Paulo's main interest in federal power was to control monetary and exchange rate policies, thereby facilitating the process of obtaining loans abroad for its coffee crops. Minas Gerais, on the other hand, had a dense population and wielded significant power, resulting in the establishment of the "Milk Coffee politics," which involved alternating presidents from both states. During the crisis, Washington Luís attempted to dismantle this arrangement, which ultimately led to Getúlio Vargas, a native of Rio Grande do Sul, assuming power.

By 1932, the people of São Paulo were particularly dissatisfied with Getúlio. This discontent was demonstrated in January when approximately 100,000 individuals gathered at Sé Square, the capital of the state, for a historic rally. News of this event spread throughout the country and reached the city of Salto, including the Stefanini household. Three months later, Dovídio left Salto to join the São Paulo artillery in preparation for the conflict that erupted on July 9, 1932. Alongside him, 200,000 men fought against Getúlio. Official reports indicate that 634 fighters died in battle, although estimates have suggested that the actual number of lives lost exceeded a thousand.

The war came to an end three months later, and Dovídio relocated to the capital of São Paulo, settling in the old Lapa neighborhood, which was populated by Venetians and Tyroleans. The rest of his family joined him later when Dovídio's sister began dating a Brazilian man from Salto. Francisco disapproved of her suitor and decided to move his family to São Paulo in an attempt to separate the couple.

Francisco worked in brickmaking, glassworks, and surveillance. He passed away in late 1944, before the end of World War II. By that time, his son Dovídio had already left Lapa and settled in Brás, a neighborhood with a significant Italian population. Other Italian families also migrated to different neighborhoods like Bexiga, which had a concentration of immigrants from Southern Italy, particularly Calabria. Bom Retiro, on the other hand, attracted the first settlers from the North, especially those from the Veneto region. However, Brás remained the neighborhood with the largest population of Italian descendants, particularly Neapolitans. It was in Brás that Milton Stefanini was born in 1938, not far from the Inn of the Immigrants, where his great-grandfather had stayed 49 years earlier.

This was a crucial period when Brazil transitioned from an agrarian society to an industrial one, and Milton experienced the peak of that era. From the late 1940s, when Milton was 10 years old, until the late 1970s, Brazil's economy grew by an average of 7% annually. It was a time of optimism, with many people investing in the future of Brazil as industrialization seemed imminent.

Milton worked for 22 years at Facas Brooklin and Aços Brooklin. In the late 1950s, at the age of 21, Milton married

Adélia Silva Stefanini. Their first child, Marco Antônio Silva Stefanini, was born a year later on December 1, 1960. Over the following years, the Stefanini family welcomed two more members, daughters Mônica and Kátia. As the family grew, they made a living.

At the beginning of the 1970s, Milton acquired a Volkswagen Beetle through a consortium and built a house on Rua Caropá in Alto de Pinheiros, a neighborhood in the western part of São Paulo. It was a hopeful moment for the family, and in 1974, Marco's parents became partners of Produtos Lampo, a pioneering company that initially manufactured metal frames and later expanded to clotheslines.

Produtos Lampo was founded fifteen years earlier by a German immigrant as a small shop in the Sé region. Five years later, it moved to Lapa, the same Italian neighborhood where Dovídio Stefanini had settled upon arriving in São Paulo. In Lapa, Milton's Produtos Lampo would experience its peak, paralleling the country's economic growth.

Milton was becoming an entrepreneur during the tail end of the period known as the Brazilian miracle. Between 1967 and 1973, Brazil's economy grew at an average rate of over 11%. However, a significant event took place in the last year of this boom: the Yom Kippur War, where Egypt and Syria attacked Israel. This event marked the beginning of a turning point, although few in Brazil could anticipate the consequences.

The impact of the Yom Kippur War was profound when the Organization of Petroleum Exporting Countries (OPEC) suspended oil exports to countries supporting Israel, including the United States and Europe. Brazil, with Petrobras being the largest buyer of oil in the world, demonstrated its external dependence. Eight out of every ten barrels consumed in the country were imported. The first oil shock in 1973 caused prices to rise, but the cost of a barrel remained relatively low, and filling up a gas tank was still affordable. It was in 1979 that cheap energy truly ended.

Despite these challenges, Brazil continued to experience growth, and the population still held onto the belief in the Brazilian miracle. This helps explain why Milton became an entrepreneur in 1974, unaware of how the Arab-Israeli war would affect Brazil's economy. However, the consequences were yet to be seen. In the six years after taking over Produtos Lampo, Dovídio's son enjoyed an annual growth rate of 7%, highlighting the excellent performance of the Brazilian economy.

While Milton took care of finances, Adélia managed the factory. Produtos Lampo employed 50 individuals and operated in two large warehouses, totaling 2,400 square meters in Lapa. The company sold clothesline products and, in some cases, provided installation services at customers' homes, with a team of twelve installers taking care of this task.

Representatives from Produtos Lampo were present in almost all Brazilian state capitals, except for some states in the North and Northeast. Even during the crisis of the 1980s when Marco was searching for a job, Milton and Adélia managed to maintain some level of success. Although their business was small, the competition was even smaller.

The market for clotheslines was peaceful, and the couple only faced problems years later due to the comfort of this crisis-free environment.

In 1984, Lampo was doing very well, but Milton didn't consider making things easier for Marco. He would provide guidance and recommend friends, but he would not pay for his children's mistakes.

The Brazilian economy was performing poorly. The effects of the global oil crisis took time to reach Brazil, but finally, in the first half of the 1980s, the pressure on fuel led automakers and the Brazilian government to bet on a different fuel. It was during this time that Marco was looking for a job with what seemed like a useless diploma in hand, and Fiat sold the first Brazilian alcohol-powered car.

Mexico's moratorium, the aid requested by the poorest countries from the IMF, a struggling Brazil with no external reserves, and Figueiredo's low popularity all sent a clear message to businessmen and the population: things are going badly, and it is not a good time to invest, let alone hire.

This was the scenario Marco faced in his senior year of college. However, at that time, his main interest was to save money to travel. He aimed to visit different places with a group of friends, typical youth from the 1980s, wearing baggy pants, citrus colors, and rubber backpacks.

During each trip, the same scene played out.

"Marco, don't tell me you want to stop at yet another museum."

"Just listen to music," he would reply.

His friend would stick the headphones of his yellow Sony Walkman into his long, gelled hair and sink into the car seat while the rest of them slept.

Although not an exceptional student, Marco took odd jobs to fund his travels. He taught judo, chemistry, physics, and whatever came his way. If he didn't know a subject, he would grab a book and study for half an hour before meeting his student.

Milton would ask him, "Marco, do you know anything about this subject?"

His son would reply, "Nothing at all. But don't worry, I'll just read a book half an hour before and wing it."

Truth be told, Marco wasn't particularly hardworking as a student. He had a reputation for being rowdy in school, always accompanied by two friends with similar behavior. Even while studying for his admission exams, he didn't put in much effort. Some say he attended the sports gymnasium more often than the classroom. At home, music played loudly, and Marco's books were scattered haphazardly throughout his room. In the morning, his younger sister, Mônica, had to take Marco's car out of the garage before leaving for work.

Apart from his apparent neglect in studies, the Stefanini family didn't have much cause for concern. Adélia had wondered whether her inquisitive and moody son would have problems with the dictatorship. However, things went smoothly for him in college, even though he frequently skipped class and spent more time in the sports gymnasium. He consistently brought home good grades.

This was common among the students of the 1980s, an era of youth in which protest signs were limited to headbands, which were now more of a reference to the sports environment and concerts like Rock in Rio.

Throughout his life, Marco took great care of his health. He avoided cigarettes, saw rock music as a form of entertainment only, and had no need to engage in political opposition.

By the end of 1983, Marco, the eldest son of the Stefanini family, graduated from USP with the grades of a scholar, not a swimmer. However, in 1984, after returning from Goiás and facing unemployment, he didn't know what to do with all the knowledge he had accumulated without much effort.

CHAPTER 2

INFORMATION

TECHNOLOGY

T he straight-haired, thin, sunburnt lad slowly opened his apartment window. That unusual malaise surprised the family, because that particular Stefanini was known for never giving up. He had wandered for ten days at the cassiterite mines in Goiás and was now back in São Paulo without knowing what to do. It was the end of his cerrado adventure.

Mining had been a frustrating experience, but Milton and Adélia were relieved to see their 23-year-old son return without contracting malaria, which was common in Goiás at the time. Despite their relief, they noticed an uncharacteristic sadness in Marco.

The Brazilian economy in 1984 seemed to reflect Marco's mood. Forecasts from Rhodia and Itaú predicted a 3% contraction in the Gross Domestic Product (GDP). The combination of his Goiás experience and the country's economic situation dampened Marco Stefanini's spirit.

However, things were not entirely bleak for the family. Milton's business, Produtos Lampo, was stable, and he considered helping his son in his own way, without making things too easy. Assistance came in the form of a broker friend who specialized in foreign trade and mentioned an American buyer interested in purchasing precious gems. Despite Marco's limited knowledge of gemology, having taken it as an optional subject at USP, the idea of exporting gems ignited his enthusiasm and lifted his "depression."

The young entrepreneur decided to acquire gemstones in Teófilo Otoni, a municipality in Minas Gerais located 450 kilometers away from Belo Horizonte. The region was known for its tourmalines, agates, amethysts, and emeralds. Marco called a friend, and together they embarked on a twelve-hour bus journey to the small city.

In February, the northeastern part of Minas Gerais was hot and humid, with clear skies. Amidst their quest for gems, the two aspiring merchants soon discovered that Teófilo Otoni was a hub for stones, and there was no need to venture out to the mines. Under the scorching sun, they walked a few blocks until they reached Avenida Getúlio Vargas, the city's main thoroughfare, lined with dozens of stores where they easily found what they were looking for. Marco and his friend purchased $500 worth of gems, with the plan to resell them for $1,000 to the American buyer. If successful, they would consider buying more in the future.

During the long bus journey back to São Paulo, Marco and his friend took the stones out of their pockets and evaluated them. They were semi-precious stones like tourmaline, topaz, and beryl. It felt like a successful adventure or, in the parlance of the time, "cool!"

Once back in São Paulo, there was one final purchase to be made. They visited Praça da República, where many people from Rio Grande do Sul had offices, and selected a geode—an enormous stone that, when cut in half, reveals an interior filled with crystals. With the acquisition of the goods complete, the American buyer accepted the offered amount and converted the $1,000 into Cruzeiros, which amounted to approximately Cr$1.4 million. That was the agreed amount for the two partners to receive, with zero risk for the buyer but a high risk for the young exporters attempting their first sale.

The sooner the American received the stones, the better, as any delay would erode their profits due to inflation. If they managed to get paid within two months, it would still be a worthwhile deal. The initial $500 invested in the stones would be worth Cr$820,000, and the two young exporters would receive Cr$1.4 million, making the transaction a success.

Marco sent the stones to the buyer in the United States and waited. At the time, only a few people exported gemstones, and the goods were held up at US customs due to missing documents. Meanwhile, Marco had to pay to store the stones at the customs warehouse. If it took any longer, all the profit would go towards paying for the storage, possibly leading to a loss.

While waiting for the gems to be cleared, Marco tried not to get upset and avoided the "bad vibes" by going to the swimming pool at USP. The sun made the water sparkle like the precious stones awaiting the kind heart of a customs official. Despite this distraction, Marco's thoughts always returned to the pressing need to earn money.

A friend heard about Marco's troubles and suggested, "How about teaching physics?" This wasn't a completely new idea, as Marco was already teaching at the Alves Cruz public school in the afternoon, filling in for their geography teacher. Taking on more classes would mean a little more money. His colleague used to teach at the Objetivo school and mentioned that they still didn't have a teacher for that subject. Desperate for money, Marco took on yet another gig and started teaching at the private school for three months.

While young Stefanini was trying to make some money, the country's economy was deteriorating. Interest rates were high, credit was tight, consumption was declining, and employment was stagnant. Things were truly dire. In January, the minimum wage, initially at Cr$ 57,120, increased by 74.8%. Expenses, such as rent, went up by 136.90%. Brazilians were finding it increasingly difficult to manage their money.

On the currency exchange front, the situation was also becoming more intense. Foreign debt had surpassed USD 100 billion, an unhealthy amount and a sign that something would soon happen to the Brazilian currency. Economists anticipated significant devaluation, which spelled bad prospects for payments in Cruzeiros and even worse for jobs.

The critical economic situation fueled the Diretas Já movement. Tancredo Neves, from the PMDB party, defeated the candidate favored by the current military regime, Paulo Maluf (PDS, currently known as Partido Progressista), in the indirect elections and became the president of the Republic. Changes were urgently needed.

One day, Marco's sister Monica came home, sat on the couch in the living room, looked at her brother, smiled, and asked, "What do you think about working with computers?" In 1984, Marco's sister worked at the Federal Data Processing Service (Serpro). She led two different lives—one as a student and the other as a systems analyst. She studied mathematics at the PUC campus in the Consolação region and commuted 15 kilometers by car between the college campus and the Serpro Information Processing Center in Osasco. It was quite a journey, but worth it for a job like that.

Marco's sister wanted to help him and believed that the field of computing held great promise. At the time, the sector was starting to gain popularity, even among younger people. Alongside desirable items like the Rubik's Cube and the Mobylette, teenagers and children played with their Ataris at home, and some even had small computers like the CP-300, the

Japanese standard MSX, and the first Apple computers. Microcomputers were the new trend.

Microinformatics also featured in the pages of Veja magazine, which offered an encyclopedia on the subject. The first issue discussed the TK-85 by Micrológica, the cheapest computer on the market, priced at 260,000 cruzeiros or 4.5 times the minimum wage. It was simply a keyboard that could be connected to a TV, but it ignited the desire of hobbyists fascinated with home computing.

The more serious side of technology was also flourishing. Professionals, such as doctors, started using computers to cross-reference patients and print exercise and diet prescriptions. They paid an average of 3 million cruzeiros for one of these devices.

For major companies, these "toys" became significant industrial investments. Itautec, created to serve the Itaú bank, had been operating in the IT sector for five years and published a two-page article in the press, showcasing the production of a medium-sized computer with national technology and IBM standards. With 72 million cruzeiros, one could purchase a computer with 8 megabytes of memory and the ability to process 2 million instructions per second.

Information technology was finally starting to generate substantial revenue in Brazil, with significant gains and losses at stake. While Marco enjoyed his time sleeping in hammocks in the Goiás countryside, President João Figueiredo shut down Empresa Digital Brasileira S.A. (Digibrás) after it incurred a loss of 1.2 billion cruzeiros. The value of the loss was enough to purchase the 22-story building of the Guanabara Palace Hotel, which was sold that same week.

Given the substantial amounts involved, IT professionals became surprisingly desirable in the Brazilian market, regardless of whether they achieved good or bad results. It was the newest and most promising field of work, and the Serpro branch where Monica worked was one of the most sought-after places. They offered cohorts with six months of training, and out of the 25 cohorts, only the best six were hired, while the rest became highly coveted hires in the market. However, the federal agency only admitted professionals with college-level education in technology-related areas, such as engineers and mathematicians. Unfortunately, as a geologist, Marco didn't stand a chance at Serpro.

That's when Monica's friend, Wang, a Chinese-Brazilian individual, told her about a course on mainframes at Bradesco bank. Marco's background in geology didn't help much, but the bank would accept any course in the exact sciences, and geology was considered part of that universe.

Once again, Monica came home and called Marco, presenting him with a more tangible offer. She asked, "So, what do you think about working with information technology?" Marco had no better alternative, especially since the gems were still stuck in the US customs office, and the value of the business was decreasing each day. Months later, the gems would be cleared, and Marco would receive the promised Cr$1.4 million. However, due to the devaluation of the Cruzeiro and inflation, the money was practically worth the same as the US$500 he had spent to buy the stones. Moreover, the time spent in customs storage cost him around USD 1,000, a significant amount for young Marco at the time. His father didn't say anything, thinking it was good that his son showed initiative, but he didn't provide any other assistance either. Marco had to bear the entire cost himself.

As a young person facing a challenge, the feeling of omnipotence gave way to doubt and insecurity. Graduates seeking their first job often feel as if they're staring into an abyss.

They can either retreat and return to the comfort of their families, which Marco didn't want, or they can move forward without knowing where they will end up. In an economic crisis, everything becomes worse, more confusing, and distressing. When young people read about crises in the newspapers, they start to believe that any effort is useless and that they have nowhere else to go. It's a total downer.

The days spent in the pale green bush of Goiás, far away from his family, the lost stones from Teófilo Otoni, the lack of money and prospects—all of it made Monica's suggestion seem like a saving grace. The starting salary at Bradesco would be much lower than what he earned teaching at Objetivo, only half as much. Even the classes had started to pay less than a geologist's salary. But Marco saw it as an opportunity for a real job, as it was money and a chance to work at a big bank.

Marco then realized that even his revolt during the Goiás adventure had been a form of youthful rebellion. Although mining ultimately proved to be a bad investment, he had complained excessively and misplayed his hand. Now, he was about to enter a new world, and this time he had to be at his best. The bank finally offered him the real possibility of a promising future. It was time to face reality in an office, the corporate universe.

Just like today, Bradesco was a powerhouse. At that time, it was more than a bank; it was an industry. Originating from a printing company where the founder, Amador Aguiar, lost the index finger of his right hand, the bank had grown into a company where everything was measured in colossal figures.

At Bradesco, every transaction was meticulously reported to clients, and the bank had an obsession with providing every detail. To ensure efficient communication, two thousand scooters and over a thousand Volkswagen Beetles and other cars were deployed from the headquarters in Osasco to transport information to clients and bank branches. The residents near Cidade de Deus, the bank's head office, were accustomed to seeing queues of trucks entering the premises. These trucks came from Bahia loaded with jacaranda lumber, which was then taken to the bank's proprietary carpentry shop. There, employees produced a thousand meters of counters each month for the bank branches. Although it wasn't exactly the company Marco had envisioned working for, Bradesco was a colossal institution in terms of its workforce and numerical figures.

In the company founded by Amador Aguiar, there was always enough money to pioneer new ventures, and this extended to its technology department as well. The first data network at Embratel was created to meet Bradesco's demand. Years later, Bradesco played a role in selling the first Brazilian electronic injection developed in the country by Bosch to Volkswagen. The bank also supported the nationalization of technology in Brazil, aiming to export value-added products rather than just relying on commodities like rough gemstones.

In the pursuit of innovation, information technology played a crucial role in making processes faster and more efficient. Initially, the bank used large computing machines such as the IBM 1401 primarily for printing purposes rather than complex calculations. Enormous amounts of paper, weighing over 60 tonnes, were printed daily, filling ten trucks. In the 1970s, calculations began to be performed using machines like the IBM 360, and the fleet of VW Beetles carrying documents was replaced with small envelopes.

The advent of technology brought a new breed of professionals to Cidade de Deus—knowledgeable individuals respected by their colleagues, skilled in working with intricate machines. The data processing department alone employed

10,000 people, including 2,500 programmers. These employees required extensive training, and Bradesco not only manufactured its own furniture for branches but also provided education.

The journey began with Olivetti, Burroughs, and Cobra machines. Workshops were even established to produce spare parts. Technicians would join Bradesco, learn, live their careers, and retire within the organization. The army of employees dedicated to maintaining the calculating machines totaled 2,500.

The individual chosen to work in information technology typically learned to read at Bradesco's schools. As children, they attended elementary school and then a technically-oriented high school, both located at Fundação Bradesco. These schools primarily catered to children of the bank's employees. Upon choosing a career in computing, they became programmers in trial programs, similar to trainees today. After a year and a half, they transitioned into full-time employment. Another year and a half later, they could expect a promotion to a senior position. Following this, they underwent another year and a half of training and were promoted to analysts in trial programs, completing a roughly ten-year educational cycle within Bradesco. It was rare for people to be fired from the organization.

An important change came for Bradesco when the president of IBM, Robeli José Libero, suggested to Bradesco's president, Lázaro Brandão, the establishment of a program for systems analysts within the bank. The goal was to attract young talent to key technical positions, indicating the beginning of the hunt for new professionals in the market.

Brandão, who had led the institution for just over three years after being directly appointed by Amador Aguiar, recognized the rapid changes in technology and the need for a different type of professional: a business analyst. These professionals understood both technology and the bank's processes, serving as a bridge between the two. Consequently, Bradesco and IBM started training analysts with a more open-minded approach, combining business and technology expertise.

For Marco, entering this world marked an awkward transition. His first task was to sign a document pledging not to engage in questionable activities or adopt an unconventional appearance. While Marco was more discreet in his style, the rules practically banned the over-the-top looks and vibrant colors of the 1980s from the classroom. From then on, Marco and his peers were allowed relatively casual clothes, but they had to wear dress pants and short-sleeved shirts. They were constantly observed by the entire bank community, including IBM consultants who were distanced from the academic world but deeply embedded in the corporate realm of information technology. It was undoubtedly a highly formal environment, quite different from the one that initially attracted Marco to geology.

Applicants for jobs at Bradesco, particularly those in the field of information technology, often had no prior knowledge of computers. Many of them came from rural areas and stayed in hotels near the bank's headquarters or in lodgings provided in Cidade de Deus for individuals from less privileged backgrounds who came from outside São Paulo.

On May 23, 1984, Marco Stefanini woke up early and embarked on a journey to Osasco, where Cidade de Deus, the Bradesco headquarters, was located. The distance from Marco's home in the Alto de Pinheiros neighborhood in São Paulo was less than 10 km. As he arrived at the gate near Avenida Iara, he entered the financial complex, passing by tall eucalyptus trees until he reached the building designated for computer classes: Centrefor.

Marco was part of the fourth class of a new generation of analysts, known as FAS 4, along with 27 other candidates. Over 70 students had already completed the course. This training program granted them entry into the corporate world of information technology, which was commonly referred to as "informatics" at that time.

During that era, most people were unfamiliar with what computers did and their practical usefulness. Despite the respect commanded by technology, the appearance of a mainframe often left people disappointed. It resembled a blue and beige box, standing six feet tall and three feet wide, akin to a small closet or a washing machine. Within it, tapes whirred away.

Entering this world of technology could be a challenging endeavor. Students had to learn abstract subjects such as logic and computer theory, which constituted the most difficult part of the three-week training course. They dedicated eight hours a day to continuous study, with different teachers for each subject, amounting to ten or eleven subjects in total. Every test brought the fear of elimination, jeopardizing the opportunity to pursue a career at Bradesco. The passing grade was 7, and failing a single test would result in automatic expulsion.

The youthful students, indulging in Supra-Sumo tablets and soft candies, stood in contrast to Bradesco's conservative culture. A significant portion of the class was perceived as monotonous, involving the reading of thick IBM manuals spanning over 500 pages. Classes began at 8 am, and lunch break commenced promptly at noon. Bradesco provided lunch and snacks for all students, and those residing in the lodging were even served breakfast and dinner. Classes resumed at 2 pm and continued until 6 pm, marking the end of the day. Students residing in the lodging were allowed to leave the school premises but had to return by 11 pm. Some students intentionally arrived ten minutes late to spend time with Bradesco girls who followed the fashion trends of the decade, characterized by large perms, flashy makeup, and colorful accessories.

The most exciting part of the course was when students could directly interact with the mainframe computers. Facing the black screen with green letters, they learned how to operate the main computer languages: Cobol and the intricate Assembly language, filled with codes incomprehensible to non-experts.

Throughout the course, Marco and his colleagues primarily utilized the same room. Located on the first floor, they would first write the program on paper before descending to the ground floor, where the laboratory equipped with terminals was situated. Working in pairs, they would test the code they had just created. The room housed fourteen terminals, half IBM and half Cobra. Everyone preferred the IBM terminals, and the latecomers were left with the Cobras. Marco was quick and efficient, always managing to secure an IBM terminal.

Tasks initially seemed deceptively simple, but all students experienced a certain amount of terror and stress. After explaining some theory about the programming language, the professor would ask them to write a trivial application. If the application worked without errors, students would receive a perfect score. However, if the software crashed, they were allowed to review the code and attempt to run it again. With each unsuccessful attempt, they would lose a mark. No student could leave the room without successfully running the software. Failure to do so resulted in a grade of zero, which meant bidding farewell to a career at the bank.

The pursuit of understanding informatics and adapting to Bradesco's culture brought about changes in young Marco

Stefanini. He became increasingly absent from his family, often tired, and his course at Bradesco proved to be more awkward, exhausting, and stressful than his college experience. The months spent searching for a job and the uncertainties and failed projects in geology now seemed distant and meaningless. The future and financial prospects lay in the corporate world, even if it meant sacrificing adventure and unconventional trips.

One of Marco's fellow classmates was Luiz Edmundo Machado, a young engineer who had reluctantly come to São Paulo from Barretos to study at Bradesco. Luiz Edmundo had no desire to work in the bustling city, but like Marco, he felt the pressure to embark on a career.

The course concluded in November 1984, and as the last lessons approached, students were eager to discover who would be ranked first in the class. The top eight students would have the privilege of choosing the area in which they would work at Bradesco. The most coveted position was technical support, as nobody understood much about computers, and the computer technicians were seen as saviors when something went wrong and the computers crashed, traversing Cidade de Deus and interacting with everyone.

The top student in the class was Nelson, a descendant of Germans known as Piu-Piu among his peers. The second-place student was Hamilton, who later left the field and went to work as a teacher in Ilha Solteira.

Marco and Luiz Edmundo had identical grades in some subjects. Marco performed better in certain areas, while Luiz Edmundo excelled in others, but their overall grades were exactly the same up to the third decimal place. Luiz Edmundo fondly referred to Marco as "Marcão." In the end, Marco secured the third position. Like his friends who also stood on the podium in the Bradesco course, the former geologist chose to join the technical support department. From the realm of geology and precious gems and the peacefulness of a hammock in the cerrado of Goiás, Marco was now firmly entering the world of information technology.

CHAPTER 3

MICRO LAND

The piece of paper crumpled on the floor for the thousandth time, falling from the printer in the mainframe room. Marco picked up the ream and went to his desk, installed in a corner of that same floor, in the middle of the cubicle where the seven members of Bradesco's capacity planning and performance team were stationed. He thought of words his father had said the night before. "Are you interested?" his father had asked. Marco's gaze fell upon the table, his eyes avoiding the sight of the long code printed in blurry ink. The weight of his decision and the challenges of his new career path weighed heavily on him in that moment.

He glanced at the partition that separated him from the rest of Bradesco's IT department. The work proceeded silently on that cold February morning in 1985, beneath the pale yellow light of offices deprived of sufficient sunshine and amidst the cold, damp air of the air conditioner. Two men in short-sleeved shirts conversed near the window, overlooking a few empty tables, while the rest of the staff focused on their screens displaying black backgrounds with green lettering. Near the entrance, a somber secretary with small glasses nodded on the phone, discussing a "meeting" and a "complicated schedule."

The planning team experienced an even greater level of tranquility. Aside from Marco, the team consisted of a senior analyst, three programmers, and the team leader. Both Marco and his classmate, Luiz Edmundo, were newcomers in their trial programs. They spent the majority of their time scanning programming codes, examining the efficiency of computer processes, and optimizing memory allocation in mainframes, among other intricate details. It was serene. Almost unnervingly so.

One significant advantage of their department was the absence of the need to rush out in the middle of the night to address system crashes, a frequent reality for those working in the highly sought-after field of technical support. Marco and Luiz Edmundo had deliberately chosen a different path and joined the planning team. This allowed them to conduct more research, which greatly appealed to Luiz Edmundo. Apart from occasional trips to the printer to check reports or examine programming routines printed on the dot matrix printer with faint letters, the team's routine mainly revolved around their meticulous work. It was a pleasant routine for those who loved tinkering with computers, professionals known as "bit brushers" – experts in manipulating the smallest unit of information in computers. Luiz Edmundo fit this description, but Marco did not.

While initially attractive, the tranquility of their work began to unsettle the young Stefanini. Having learned to operate large computers during the Bradesco program, he believed, at the age of 23, that information technology held great promise. However, his mind often wandered far beyond the walls of Cidade de Deus.

"Would you like a job?" Milton Stefanini's voice resounded once again, shaking Marco from his thoughts.

Bradesco's capacity and performance planning area was situated in the bank's newly constructed building, just across the street from Centrefor. Some of the mainframes, specifically the IBM 3033s acquired in 1979, were housed there. Initially, the older IBM 4381 and IBM 4041, comprising three or four mainframes, handled all of the bank's information processing.

As Bradesco expanded, new machines were added, necessitating the recruitment of more personnel.

The career progression for these new professionals was slow, frustratingly slow for an ambitious young man like Marco. Those accepted into the program, such as Marco and Luiz Edmundo, who already held university degrees, became analysts in trial programs within six months. However, many left before completing a year, and some even departed after only four months. Consequently, some bank employees began referring to potential defectors as "mercenaries."

Despite earning over two million cruzeiros a month for their work, it was not a significant amount considering the inflation of the time. Many people had become millionaires due to the devalued currency. Nevertheless, for Marco and Luiz Edmundo, the number of zeros in their paycheck still made them feel like millionaires. However, Marco desired more. While Luiz, the engineer, had a genuine passion for information technology and working with mainframes, Marco saw the bank as a vast pool of opportunities—a typical entrepreneur.

However, this ambitious entrepreneur encountered opportunities he couldn't fully embrace. Despite the buzz surrounding information technology, it didn't involve the large computers Marco had mastered. The first personal computers were beginning to emerge in Brazil, small devices connected to TVs and sold in supermarkets. Though they were still considered niche products, attracting only a small group of individuals interested in the field of microinformatics, their popularity was steadily growing. The first applications for these smaller machines were being sold to medium-sized companies, all of which existed outside the realm of Bradesco, in a world called Micro land.

As Marco observed the tranquility of Bradesco's IT department, his mind was occupied with thoughts of the vast opportunities beyond those walls. The day before, Milton had called Marco for a chat, and during the conversation, he posed a question: "Are you interested in a job outside Bradesco?" No matter the specifics, Marco's interest was piqued. The year 1985 seemed poised to offer more than just a future within Bradesco.

Here's the situation: Marco's father knew the owner of a chain of construction material stores, and they were intrigued by the potential of this new technology in software and computers. Their idea was to use personal computers to manage the company's inventory and payments. However, developing such a system required expertise in a high-level language—one that closely resembled human language and was well-suited for creating commercial systems. Marco lacked in-depth knowledge in these areas, but he knew someone who possessed the necessary expertise.

João Jorge Galin had attended the same course and belonged to the same class as Marco at Bradesco, FAS 4. Unlike Marco, who had studied geology and stumbled into the tech field by chance, João Jorge was an engineer by profession. With a father who owned a business and a brother who was also an engineer, João Jorge pursued civil engineering at USP and graduated at the age of 24 in 1976. In 1977, seven years before his graduation from Bradesco, he became a public servant and worked in urban planning for the state government of São Paulo for five years. However, he found the work monotonous and repetitive. Drawing on his engineering background, he sought to introduce standardization and automation to the field. When he grew tired of urban planning, João Jorge managed to convince his colleagues at Prodesp to open an internship position in a completely different line of work: informatics.

In 1983, João Jorge began familiarizing himself with microcomputers, despite having no prior experience with these machines. While interning at Prodesp, he learned about the course at Bradesco through a friend's son and decided to take a chance. Instead of pursuing a career managing large mainframes, João Jorge chose to continue working with microcomputers at Bradesco. When Marco called his colleague and explained the opportunity outside of Bradesco, he asked João Jorge if he would be willing to help. João Jorge saw it as a chance to gain valuable experience in computer technology, even if it was different from his work at Bradesco. Thus, the two friends embarked on developing systems for a small company.

They would spend nights and weekends working on an application for a chain of construction material stores, with Marco learning to code in dBase II. Leaving Bradesco together, they would relax and slightly loosen their formal shirts, a classic 1980s attire with the top buttons undone, and immerse themselves in coding. Working without a hard drive and relying on floppy disks, they built a system capable of handling up to five thousand product items. João Jorge enjoyed the experience, had a few beers, learned what he wanted, and returned his focus to Bradesco.

However, Marco had a different perspective. Money was tight, the nights weren't exactly enjoyable, and he didn't particularly enjoy programming. Yet, for some reason, this venture seemed to hold more possibilities than a career in the bank. It was a difficult decision to make. On one hand, there was the largest Brazilian bank, a financial powerhouse offering stable and respectable employment, not to mention the massive systems handling impressive sums of money. On the other hand, there was a small adventure with no guarantees, a job for a smaller company using small computers, and even lower pay.

For almost a year, Marco continued his routine at the bank without taking on any outside jobs. However, work started to bother him. Shortly before completing two years in his role, he learned about a job opening at Engesa, an industrial company in the military defense sector that had recently moved its headquarters to Barueri. Although smaller than Bradesco, this group of companies operated in various segments of the economy and exported to 37 countries. It was a bit farther from Marco's home in Alto de Pinheiros, but in return, he would have a more flexible work environment in terms of business affairs and working hours. In August 1986, Marco accepted the proposal, and his entrepreneurial spirit found a bit more freedom.

However, Marco quickly realized that even the work at Engesa did not truly matter to him. The flexible hours allowed him to continue pursuing odd jobs and earning money. He could now teach and take on other systems proposals. But his quest for opportunities would not be easy. After his experience with João Jorge in the chain of stores, Marco went through a long period without programming.

At home, Milton and Adélia were aware that their son was seeking opportunities. One day, towards the end of 1986, a few months after Marco joined Engesa, Adélia was talking to her supplier and friend, Claudino Frignani, the owner of Azul Plast, a company that sold plastic materials for Produtos Lampo. Like Milton, Claudino was the son of an oriundi, which created a bond between the families. During their conversation, amidst a negotiation, Claudino and Adélia discussed their children. They mentioned that Marco was looking for ventures in information technology, while Claudino's daughter, Cristina, wanted to digitize Azul Plast. It seemed like a perfect match.

It wasn't a big company, with 50 employees that year, but information technology was really starting to catch on among smaller firms. Azul Plast had been founded in 1964 by Claudino, and his daughter Cristina helped him manage it, along with two other brothers. They produced flexible PVC pipes and other plastics, and unlike Produtos Lampo, they felt the pressure of the market. At the time, Claudino and his children supplied directly to the automobile industry, with General Motors and Honda (motorcycles) as their main customers. However, systems managers – suppliers stationed in the factory – tended to deal with automakers and Azul Plast was about to be subcontracted. The pressure for a lower price and higher quality would be greater; the strength of the small business among automakers, weaker.

To make matters worse for any businessperson, the Cruzado Plan was already considered dead in the ground, shortly after PMDB's victory in the state elections. After nine months of boosting price premiums, the government announced historic increases in public tariffs on fuel and car prices in the second version of the Cruzado Plan. Marco and Cristina used to fill their gas tanks paying just over 180 Cruzados. After the elections, they started spending almost 300. The Chevette Sedan, the cheapest car in the country, went from 50,000 Cruzados to 90,000. The inflation, previously under momentary control, was accelerating and would reach 62% in the aggregate for the year.

Within Azul Plast, the search for efficiency increased in a moment of pure economic instability. By then, Cristina, aged 29, had done all the financial administration manually. The finances area comprised just her, and this menial task took up almost all of her time. Despite the slight respite from inflation at the start of the Cruzado Plan, entrepreneurs already knew that they needed to deal with an environment in which prices were changing almost daily. No one could lose sight of the bills for even a day.

Early in the morning, Cristina checked the company's balance at three banks and verified what had been paid. Usually, they were a payment short, and she would have to add and subtract for hours in order to find out what was missing. Then, she had to check her accounts payable so she could sign checks, charge customers, and still find time to type up pay slips. At best, at midday she managed to send an errand boy to the three banks. In the time she had left, she took care of the personnel department and of the accounting.

It may sound like a paradox, but the beneficial effect of a crisis is precisely that it makes bad situations intolerable. Inflation added to the difficulties of the small entrepreneur and made management a difficult effort to bear. If a machine could make life easier, it would be most welcome.

Cristina's first contact with information technology was in 1983, when she insisted that Claudino should buy an Itautec computer. Her father would never touch a computer, but the machine was about to change his daughter's routine. That first Itautec came with some applications like Lotus, but the girl couldn't use anything, even with the help of tech support. Three years later, while Marco was at Engesa, Cristina bought a generic, unbranded PC and decided once again to computerize Azul Plast's financial department. She needed a system for accounts payable, receivable, and cash flow. That was precisely what her father said to Adélia, Marco's mother.

The company was located in the South Zone, a few blocks away from Marginal Pinheiros, next to companies like Monark and Tinken. One night, after working at Engesa, Marco went there to talk to Cristina. They discussed the company's problem within minutes and started chatting. They were promising youths, but with empty pockets. – "I don't have money to go anywhere," Marco would say, nostalgic for the travels of his teenage years, all paid for by the odd jobs he always did. Now, even with the money from Engesa and the classes he still taught, there was almost nothing left. The change would come in good time. With the deal closed, it was time to sit down and start typing lines of code.

Several nights a week, he would go to the Azul Plast factory to develop the system, sometimes on Saturdays as well. Marco gradually understood each basic process in the operation of a company, an odd type of knowledge for a geologist. Cristina needed reports such as the bills that were about to become due, sometimes in alphabetical order, other times in order of maturity. Or even the bills for the day.

Throughout the first half of 1987, the routine repeated itself. Marco would leave Engesa, still wearing the corporate clothes of the time, with his dress shirt tucked inside his jeans, drive 25 kilometers on Marginal Pinheiros and spend the nights at Azul Plast. After six months, the system was ready. Cristina now had all the data she needed within minutes; all she had to do was press a button to see the report come out. She later hired a company to continue the computer work. The following year, the Frignani family opened their second factory and, a few years later, the third – they survived Collor's market opening effort and now supply directly once again to automakers such as Chrysler, Mercedes, Honda, and even Ford all over the world.

Marco's system was, therefore, great for Cristina, and a unique experience for the geologist. However, spending six months programming during nights and weekends inside closed doors did not seem to be an effective way to earn money. It wasn't Bradesco, it wasn't Engesa, it wasn't even Microlândia's systems.

In that year, 1987, squeezed between the codes of Azul Plast and Engesa, a certain activity became increasingly important. It was a craft that brought together everything Marco had done in his life, a synthesis of all his skills and desires. It would be the answer for the future of the Stefanini name.

CHAPTER 4

THE TANK AND TIME

A n early 43 tonnes of metal moved silently. The driver, drenched in the smell of diesel oil, drove the tank towards the back of the warehouse, while another man, at the top, tested the cannon's movement. Impressed, Marco watched the great promise that was the Osório tank as he hurried to Engesa's office.

The month was ending. It was a Friday, the eve of the dead week of Carnival 1987. It seemed about to rain, and the nearly 40 degrees Celsius were a hassle. It was better to stay inside the R&D Center, protected by the air conditioning, than inside those armored vehicles where the test pilots would sweat profusely and reek of diesel.

Here, we must bring the story back to before Marco developed the Azul Plast system, when you, the reader, will discover the important event that took place in that tumultuous year. The computer guy who didn't want to be an engineer now worked for the defense industry Engesa, a manufacturer of armored vehicles, jeeps, and trucks. Its offerings included the Cascavel reconnaissance car, the Urutu soldier transportation vehicle, the Ogum light armored car, the famous Engesa jeep, and the Osório tank prototype, which in a few months was due to be shipped to Saudi Arabia.

Meanwhile, Marco was running computers.

In economic terms, the year 1987 reserved yet another crisis for Brazil. On that same hot Friday, February 20, President José Sarney went on TV and told the people that he would not pay the foreign debt. There were over 700 creditor banks with a debt of USD 121 billion, and Brazil officially had less than USD 4 billion in reserves (unofficially, it was said that the reserve was even smaller, something like USD 500 million, which is chump change for an entire country). In practice, Brazil went bankrupt, and the way out was to default. Without even being able to use the word moratorium, the president warned that anyone who criticized the decision would be acting against the homeland. Sarney said this morsel on prime time television: "No betrayal."

In one day, the dollar jumped from 27 cruzados to 35 cruzados, and even paying dearly, nobody managed to find the currency in the market. With the default, the economy slowed to the same pace as when Marco was looking for a job in early 1984. One month after Sarney went on TV, General Motors paralyzed half of its factory. Sectors such as chemicals and pharmaceuticals recorded a 20% dip in orders. The industry was stagnant.

At Engesa, Marco's job was preserved, but the future was uncertain. Besides, running a vehicle company's computers wasn't an exciting career yet, at least not for a restless spirit.

That scenario would produce the momentum and energy for a turnaround. And it would be in that same year.

After the months of March and April, things continued at a standstill and without prospects. One night, Marco came home and received a message. A certain Nilson Vasconcelos, from a company called Servimec, had called him. He was told to call back in the evening. That was odd because it was past 8 pm, but he still made the call. On the other end, he heard a voice:

Servimec, good evening!

Nilson, then, answered the call and, without further ado, invited Marco to teach information technology classes. Marco was surely no expert on the subject yet, but these details had certainly never stopped him before. Teaching had always been a part of his life. He didn't need anything else; just himself and a subject he could learn quickly and then pass on the knowledge to others. Always as a side job, a way to fund his desires and travels.

Early in college, he gave judo lessons. His students were children from the Casulo kindergarten, located on Capote Valente street, between Rebouças and Artur Azevedo. There, he would meet his girlfriend Graça, at a party for parents and students, at the end of 1980. Nothing came out of it at first, but soon after, in 1981, he asked the girl out. They were practically the same age. Graça had arrived from Bauru three years earlier (in 1978) to attend the third year of high school and study psychology. She also graduated in 1983, like Marco, and soon got an internship, which made the boyfriend more eager to start a career.

During college, Marco continued to make a living by teaching at state-owned and private schools. After college, while working at Bradesco, he gave night classes once or twice a week and still found some time to relax. Throughout this period, teaching meant dealing with teenagers and teaching subjects that were relatively easy for a geologist. When he started to develop the systems – first with João Jorge, then at Azul Plast – Marco was forced to give fewer classes at Colégio Alves Cruz. Time had become a rarer, scarcer commodity that could readily be turned into money.

As a result, a new branch of education emerged, created by the demand in the market for a modality of knowledge unheard of at the time. Just like in Bradesco, many major corporations were heavily dependent on those new machines. There was an urgent need to train hundreds of thousands of people to operate all those systems. There was no time to wait for technicians; they had to be made from existing workers.

Demand grew, and Servimec became the largest technology school in Brazil. No one taught more students than they did, whether in one-year courses on Cobol or short technical seminars. At the start of 1987, Nilson was looking for specialists from universities and executives who ran technology companies. That was when Marco received the call.

Nilson worked for Antonio Barrio, a paulista born in Poços de Caldas who arrived in the São Paulo capital city in 1942 at the age of 6. He started working in commerce at the age of 12 and two years later joined an office of the Votorantim group. He also worked at Banco Nacional de Minas for seven years before finally moving to Burroughs, where he learned about information technology and worked for 11 years.

In 1969, Barrio bought a service company called Servimec from two Germans. It was located in the São Paulo neighborhood of Bom Retiro, on Rua Afonso Pena, and ended up becoming the largest bureau for borrowers of the National Housing Bank. It served banks, stock funds, and city halls. It competed with major processing bureaus such as IBM, Cetil, Proconsult, and ADP.

When real estate companies were strong, Servimec dominated the market. Then, the banks decided that processing information was profitable and strategic and set up their own processing centers. Barrio faced his business crisis as a personal one, betting on another niche.

In the early 1980s, Barrio entered the teaching segment and set up shop in a building on Rua Correia dos Santos, in front of a synagogue (today, the street is called Leibovitz). They started by teaching the Cobol language.

Barrio's philosophy deserves an aside. At Servimec, all students were aces, and no one could leave school without learning. It might sound like a salesman's pitch, but the truth was that students actually attended classes – as many as

41

necessary – until they understood the trade, without having to pay anything extra. If there were any freeloading rascals, Barrio preferred to ignore them.

If students came from afar, Barrio would arrange for their stay and plane tickets. If they had no money at all, Barrio would have a talk with them. In ten years, Servimec would train more than 12,000 people in that building on Correia dos Santos.

Classes were held on the fourth and last floor of the building, served by a single elevator that sometimes broke down. Barrio insisted on having someone wait for students on the top floor with a glass of juice. On Saturday afternoons, Servimec gathered children for computer classes, providing hot dogs and clowns.

Barrio's main customers were corporate human resources departments. He signed contracts and sourced students with these companies. Soon after, Barrio saw an opportunity to teach shorter but more advanced level classes. These were the technical seminars of informatics or STI. To run this new area, he called his friend Nilson Vasconcelos, with whom he had worked at Burroughs.

However, in order to get STI started, Barrio needed something that would grab the tech market's attention. He needed an international figure, not just a Brazilian expert. At the time, one of the most respected names in the world was Frenchman Jean-Dominique Warnier, who had spent over 25 years among computers and had written books on programming logic that were popular globally. Barrio invited Warnier, and he accepted, becoming the famous teacher for the inaugural class of STIs.

But Barrio also wanted to impress executives who didn't know Warnier or understand much about technology. He hired an advertising agency called London and produced an ad catalog that looked more like an art book. That catalog would impress the market a decade later.

The inaugural class took place at the Caesar Park hotel, located on Rua Augusta at the time. Over 100 people gathered in the auditorium to see and hear Warnier, with his broad forehead, oval glasses, and a small-knotted tie. With Warnier, Servimec began offering technical IT seminars, and throughout the year, the market would talk about the Frenchman's lecture.

From then on, Barrio would seek out top experts in specific subjects, whether logic or Cobol, and have them teach two- or five-day courses to select groups of corporate employees. There was a demand for these courses, and the money was there.

The first classes were also held at the Correia dos Santos address. Later on, Barrio began renting a floor of the famous Dacon building at the intersection of Avenida 9 de Julho and Avenida Cidade Jardim. The seminars had a smaller audience compared to the Correia dos Santos courses, with almost half the attendance. These short courses, lasting a few days, had at most 40 people in attendance. Many of them were returning alumni, taking their second, third, or even fourth course. Despite the smaller number of participants, the STI courses were more profitable than the Cobol courses.

Therefore, it would also be more profitable for Marco to teach the technical seminars. They went by quickly and paid well. However, it was a big challenge as the students were already employed in the IT area, often with ten or twenty years of experience. It was quite different from teaching teenagers and children.

With this new audience came a new appearance for Marco. After leaving Bradesco, he no longer needed to maintain a clean-shaven or impeccable beard. Due to lack of time, he let his beard grow, trimming it on occasion. Thus, with a thick beard that made him look older, Marco entered that first class at Servimec in May 1987, carrying a sheaf of inkjet-printed transparent paper. He faced twenty-nine students.

For Barrio and Nilson, finding teachers for the basic information technology courses was relatively easy. However, as they ventured into more advanced programs, they struggled to find experts to teach those classes. This led Nilson to invite Marco, who was knowledgeable in basic theory, to teach increasingly challenging courses. While Marco excelled in theory, teaching practical tasks like installing a virtual machine on a mainframe proved to be a new and unfamiliar experience for him.

The challenges didn't end there. Marco began receiving invitations to teach in other states, which meant he had to rush to the airport, studying the course material during the flight to familiarize himself with topics he had never seen before.

After his time at Servimec, Marco started teaching at other schools such as the São Paulo Institute, JMS, and Compucenter, the latter two being schools affiliated with IBM. Eventually, Compucenter requested that Marco leave JMS to secure exclusivity with IBM, and he agreed.

Even with the priority given to Compucenter, Marco's days remained hectic. He took time off from his work at Engesa, took leaves of absence, and did everything possible not to refuse a teaching opportunity. He would head to Rua Tutoia, where the impressive IBM building with its dark-tinted glass had been inaugurated a little over a decade earlier. On the eighth floor, overlooking Avenida 23 de Maio, Marco taught courses in the morning and afternoon. These courses were short, lasting four and a half days, from Monday morning until Friday at lunchtime.

In 1987, Marco's life underwent a transformation. Amidst the chaos of traveling, handing out course materials, and managing older students, he realized he wanted to marry Graça. He set the date for December 5th, knowing that their honeymoon would only be a quick weekend in Campos do Jordão, as he had to return to give an important two-week course at Servimec that he couldn't refuse.

Despite the economic crisis and his limited time, Marco remained determined. However, Engesa, his employer, began to pose a significant obstacle. The workload increased, and he had to take vacations to teach the courses. Sometimes, he worked overtime to exchange those extra hours for time off to teach.

Eventually, the situation became unsustainable. Towards the end of 1987, Marco found time to study French, and it was during these classes that he met the wife of the owner of the construction company Triedro. He convinced the owners to purchase a payment control system, adding yet another activity to his already busy life. This opportunity wasn't driven by a passion for software; it was just another odd job.

In November of that year, Brazilian businessmen were observing the dispute between Scopus, a Brazilian manufacturer, and Microsoft. The government attempted to enforce a reservation policy for information technology, but Brazilian software was inferior and three times more expensive than foreign alternatives. The fierce competition in the software market and the threat of trade sanctions from the US government forced Marco to consider his options.

He realized that teaching was the most promising path in his professional life so far. Although he could have pursued a career as a major executive at Bradesco or Engesa, or even become the head of a software company, which seemed unpromising at that time, Marco's true desire was to work with people. It wasn't about avoiding having a boss or being accountable to others; he knew that starting a company would entail being accountable to a lot more people and potentially making his life even more complex.

In November 1987, Marco made the decision to quit his job at Engesa as IBM's program at Compucenter offered a reasonable volume of classes that paid better than his salary at the company. As fate would have it, Engesa faced financial troubles in the following years, leading to its eventual bankruptcy. The company's problems stemmed from Iraq's default of USD 200 million and the failure to sell the heavy Osório tanks, which had absorbed all of Engesa's reserves. Marco's choice to venture into entrepreneurship by teaching IT courses independently turned out to be the right decision.

With his transition to becoming a businessman, Marco realized the need to establish his own company. While he may not have required an office, a sign on the door, or a secretary at that time, he understood the importance of officially opening a business under his name. Thus, he chose to name the company after his own family name, Stefanini. The name carried historical significance, tracing back to its origins in Italy in the 17th century, then migrating to the São Paulo countryside, participating in the 1932 Revolution, and residing in Lapa, Brás, and Bom Retiro.

On November 23, 1987, just eight days before Marco's 27th birthday, Stefanini issued its first invoice to the São Paulo Institute. The service provided was mainframe programming classes, for which the payment amounted to 6,606.84 cruzados, equivalent to approximately 110 US dollars at the time. This payment represented a little over two minimum wages.

The inception of Stefanini IT Solutions marked the beginning of Marco's entrepreneurial journey, and things appeared to be going well for him at that time.

CHAPTER 5

THIRD-PARTIES

A crowd formed around the TV set, which faced the street in a bar next to Trianon Park. Avenida Paulista slowed down to witness a financial hijacking. On the screen, Zélia Cardoso de Mello stammered and explained how the newly sworn-in government had confiscated the people's money. At her side, Ibrahim Eris was chain-smoking. Moving away from the crowd surrounding the TV, a man in a tie paced to the nearby bank, the first of many to rush to empty the ATMs. In the opposite direction, Marco crossed the street, his stomach still full from lunch and turning wildly, walking back to the Itatiaia Building. He thought about the salary of the instructors at Stefanini, trapped in the bank. He had nothing.

As usual, Brazil had actually waited to start the year of 1990 in the first days of March, after Carnival, and the population was optimistic. Collor was the first Brazilian president elected by direct vote in 25 years. Brazilians, including Marco, believed the year would be excellent. Stefanini, with just over two years of operation, had 30 corporate courses already scheduled at the start of the year.

On March 11, 1990, Marco's year began for real. That Sunday, his car, a Parati station wagon, was stolen. Soon after, on Wednesday, the day before Collor took office, the Central Bank declared a bank holiday. Here and there, a certain nervousness was setting in, a fear that investments and even savings could be confiscated. On Thursday, Zélia went on national television to announce what few people could have imagined: everything, including checking accounts, would be confiscated. Collor was hijacking 80% of the nation's assets. The inflation would subside, but the economy froze.

Stefanini's start had been rough, but there was never a lack of opportunities for growth. After issuing the first invoice at the end of 1987, Marco continued to look for opportunities. Shortly after opening the company, he met Carlos, the husband of a friend of his wife, Graça. He operated design programs on PCs and teamed up with Marco to provide training in that area as well. The first edition of the Meio & Mensagem magazine was designed by the two of them and by Marco's younger sister, Kátia, who had chicken pox on the final editing week. It all worked out in the end.

After the inaugural invoice, Marco decided to become a true businessman. In 1988, he and his new partner Carlos decided to rent a place that would be both an office and a classroom. Marco chose Avenida Paulista, the central business hub in the largest financial metropolis in Latin America.

Having chosen the region, he visited a room in the Itatiaia Building, on the corner of Avenida Paulista and Rua Padre João Manuel, right next to the Conjunto Nacional shopping center. Four elevators led to 23 small cubicles that could welcome all kinds of professionals and small businesses. In one of them, at the back, overlooking Alameda Santos and with just 38 square meters, Stefanini physically began to offer its classes. Carlos left the company soon after, but the office remained.

The cubicle contained a classroom and a reception area. In order to save space, a table was bolted to the wall. In the third class, the instructor, Graça, and five students entered the room. From the window, they could see trees and the houses on Alameda Santos. The air was thick; even the instructor had a bead of sweat running down his forehead. Graça approached the teacher and whispered:

– Don't say anything about the heat, alright?

At the start, services such as layout for publications continued to be carried out between classes by interns who stayed at the Paulista office. But what truly piqued Marco's interest was getting training contracts for major companies. His focus remained: dealing with people.

It was the start of a student hunt. Graça would take any company phone number that she could and spend the day calling and asking who the IT manager was. Marco would come back from his classes at IBM, Servimec, and others with a list of people and telephone numbers. Afterwards, they mapped out potential invitees in the companies. Any employee would do; if they got a manager, even better.

On class days, Graça arrived early at the office, cleaned up everything, swept the floor, wiped down the tables and each chair, and left the place sparkling. On each desk, she placed a piece of chocolate. There were twelve seats, but the courses/lectures were given to eight, six, or even four people.

The strategy started working, and by 1989, Marco had closed 15 deals with companies to teach his courses, with even better expectations for the following year. Some courses were paid for in advance, and by the middle of the year, 30 of them were planned. With the seizure, Collor changed everything.

Withdrawals from savings accounts were limited to 50,000 Cruzados Novos. It would be something like 6,000 or 8,000 reais in 2010 values, depending on the adjustment index used. In most cases, it was enough to feed oneself, pay rent, and other obligations. For budding entrepreneurs like Marco, no cash meant no dice.

Theoretically, the money would be returned adjusted for inflation 18 months later. There would be no loss if there were no inflation. Of course, that's not what happened, and many people lost nearly everything. But it was even worse for those who had sold properties. Or for people who, like Marco, had to pay their staff.

The entire corporate education market felt the impact. At Servimec, owned by Antonio Barrio, dozens of courses were canceled. For Marco, things were far more dramatic. All the money he had received and carefully saved was frozen by Collor. And the amounts saved to pay the instructors that March were also frozen. Of the 30 planned courses, only one remained, for the Johnson & Johnson company, which would only pay Marco 90 days later. To increase the size of the hole, there was also an unusual situation in the life of the young businessman: he acquired debts when he took an opportunity and bought two apartments at cost.

Giving up on the contracts, on the company, going back to Bradesco... That was no longer an option for Marco. The way out was to double down on the future of the business. Then, on some occasions, he expanded the strategy of teaching for free and successively began to give lectures without charging anything, a practice still employed by Stefanini today.

The lectures lasted half a day, either in the morning or in the afternoon. Getting around the city, however, became a problem since his Parati had been stolen days before the money was hijacked. The company responsible for the car's insurance arranged it so that they wouldn't pay for the claim, and Marco would end up going six months without a car. He had to rely on public transportation to get to the companies and give classes for free. ACNielsen was also located on Avenida Paulista, but it was closer to where the Paraíso subway station currently stands. The green line did not exist yet, but he could get there by bus or even on foot.

Prodam was harder to reach, as the data processing company was located in the Ibirapuera neighborhood. For Marco, taking a bus was no problem at all. However, teaching classes was a way of building relationships with the executives, and there was something peculiar about a business owner arriving on a... minibus.

Having scheduled the lecture, he took the bus. He arrived early, before everyone else, and waited for the room to fill up. He talked about analyzing mainframe performance, about everything he could offer Prodam, and what he could teach its employees. In the end, he waited for the last person to leave, shuffled through his papers, and slowly closed his folder. He waited a little longer, then went out into the hallway and stood there until the area was empty. He left Prodam, looked around, and headed for the bus stop.

Soon after the Collor administration stole all the money, Marco personally gave up to 60 free lectures to potential clients. For several of them, he would take the bus and repeat the same juggling act so that no one would see the businessman riding a minibus. A few months later, he bought a lease on a Saveiro pickup truck that his father couldn't afford and got rid of his embarrassing predicament.

Even with all the effort, however, it turned out to be a bad year; Marco made less than USD 100,000, mostly from training programs. After all expenses, it wasn't much. Worse, there was a lot of uncertainty involved – it was a seasonal service. It sold well from March to November; less so from December to February.

Despite the difficult year, Stefanini was not in the red. However, that situation could not continue. Although he did not wish to stop giving classes, Marco needed to change the business recipe, to add something to that formula. Before another crisis could end the dream.

***

The year 1990 also seemed promising for São Paulo native Odair Barrence. An IT manager at Nitro Química Brasileira, he had been with the company since he was 18. It was his first serious job. He started as an office assistant in 1969 and got to know information technology four years later when Nitro Química set up a data processing center. Odair witnessed the arrival of mainframes, printers, and their hundreds of meters of continuous form sheets printed at 300 lines per minute.

However, the long stay at Nitro Química was almost imposed on him since the place was a part of Odair's history long before he was born. Not just for him; the company had a major impact on the lives of thousands of people and was crucial for the development of Brazilian industry. More than a mere factory, Nitro Química was fundamental for Brazil's economy, for national business management, and was a classic and impressive example of a school that Odair himself would end up helping to dismantle.

This story, which affected millions of Brazilians, began in the 1930s. That was when industrialist Horácio Lafer, shortly after being elected congressman, read in a newspaper about the end of the North American factory Tubize Chatillon Corporation. It was early 1935, and the United States was still suffering from the economic crisis that began in 1929. Lafer saw a great opportunity in that.

The United States factory could be the chance to turn the tide in Brazilian industry. In the previous decade, the textile market witnessed the arrival of the first fiber, a kind of artificial silk named rayon. However, the only producer was Count Francisco Matarazzo, on whom the entire market depended, which

52

generated fantastic profits for the entrepreneur. In 1934, however, Matarazzo's patent expired, and Lafer started getting ready to produce the fiber himself, not only for rayon but also for the entire chain of products and chemical components that would come with the artificial thread.

After reading the newspaper, Lafer quickly got in touch with the Klabin cousins and businessman José Ermírio de Moraes, who had been waiting for some time for this opportunity and for Matarazzo's patent to run out. The group of industrialists also called banker Numa de Oliveira and a dozen more partners to join the deal, a gigantic and unprecedented task: to bring an entire factory with 18,000 tonnes of equipment from the United States and put it into operation in Brazil. Lafer called the Americans, who were interested in the offer, and in mid-1935, the deal was settled.

Tubize was not just a simple United States factory. It was an industrial conglomerate consisting of a spinning mill, plants for different acids, and factories for several substances. The entire factory was disassembled and placed inside ships to be transported to Brazil in one trip. To optimize space, special bricks were used inside the chemical tanks, which some consider to be the first known containers. The factory was reassembled in São Miguel Paulista, a region with historical significance and affordable land prices due to its location near the Tietê River.

The newly established factory in São Miguel Paulista became the most important in Brazilian industry. Getúlio Vargas, the Brazilian president at the time, referred to it as the "CSN of the chemical sector" within the industrialization project of the New State. Even Getúlio Vargas Filho, his son, was hired to work there as a technician in the research laboratory. Dozens of American technicians accompanied the factory, installing the machinery, training the workforce, and residing in a region that became known as Vila Americana.

The vertically integrated structure of Nitro Química allowed it to produce everything in-house, including a foundry and a sulfuric acid plant for the production of viscose thread. The factory was designed with workshops for mechanical and electrical repairs, carpentry, and a foundry. When a part broke, it was impossible to wait for imports, so designers would sketch out the part, and it would be manufactured at Nitro Química. The company even made its own furniture, including cleats for its soccer team, wooden spoons for the cafeteria, and other items needed for self-sufficiency.

For many decades, Nitro Química provided not only employment but also essential services to its employees. The Ermírio de Moraes family built a hospital nearby, where many employees saw their children born. Midwives, like Dona Geni, assisted in births in houses located just a few minutes from the factory. As Nitro Química thrived in São Miguel Paulista, Marco's grandfather, Dovídio Stefanini, had already left Salto and settled in São Paulo, where he registered the birth of Milton Stefanini.

Ten years after the factory's arrival in Brazil, Aurelino de Araújo, an immigrant from the Northeast with indigenous features and the grandfather of Odair Barrence, joined Nitro Química. He started working as a watchman in 1945, at the end of World War II, and the following year, his son-in-law Júlio followed suit and also became a watchman at the company.

During the 1950s, the landscape of São Miguel Paulista began to change as the industrialization of Brazil progressed. Nitro Química, at its peak, employed around eight thousand people and had become a significant industrial compound in the area. However, in the 1960s, under the leadership of the Ermírio de

Moraes family, certain areas of the company started to be shut down. Fábio Raváglia, representing the Ermírio de Moraes family, presided over the board of Nitro Química and made the decision to close down sections such as the foundry, knitting factory, boiler shop, and eventually the carpentry shop in 1965. This meant that Júlio, Odair's father, had to find a new job as Nitro Química was no longer engaged in furniture production.

Despite these changes, Nitro Química continued its operations until the arrival of the third generation. Ermírio Pereira de Moraes, the youngest son of José Ermírio de Moraes, known as "the Senator," had a daughter named Ana Helena who was born within the factory premises. Ana Helena and her brother Ricardo Ermírio de Moraes, who was born in 1959, represented the third generation of the family. They lived in a house inside the factory as children. In 1983, Ricardo graduated as an engineer while Marco Stefanini graduated as a geologist, both facing the challenges posed by the economic crisis in Brazil.

In 1986, Ricardo's uncle, Antonio Ermírio de Moraes, ran for the position of governor of São Paulo. The following year, Ricardo assumed the role of leading Nitro Química, a complex task for a young engineer who had just graduated. The production of rayon and the operation of the factory posed significant challenges, compounded by expensive labor costs and strong unions like the Central Única dos Trabalhadores (CUT). Ricardo had to outsource various sectors due to the dire economic circumstances.

By 1988, when Ricardo took charge of Nitro Química, the company employed five thousand people. Inflation, global competition, union pressures, and technological advancements necessitated significant changes. Ricardo reorganized the company into strategic units and outsourced non-core activities. It was during this period, in 1990, that Odair Barrence, representing the third generation of the Barrence family, joined Nitro Química. Odair worked under the CFO and reported to Ricardo.

Odair, along with his father Júlio and their family, lived just five blocks away from Nitro Química, making their commute to the factory incredibly short. Odair pursued his education at Cruzeiro do Sul University, located near the factory, where many Nitro Química employees also studied. He obtained a Bachelor's Degree in Administration and later specialized in information systems at Mauá University.

Nitro Química was the first company within the Votorantim group to introduce computers in 1973. In 1985, Odair assumed the role of head of the systems area at Nitro Química. The company had two other major areas: IT support and organization and methods. These areas were responsible for translating user requirements into corresponding flowcharts. In February 1988, the general technology manager left the company, and an external executive was hired as part of a strategy to bring fresh talent to the organization. Although they wanted Odair to remain in the company due to his extensive knowledge of the systems, he was not offered the role of department head.

However, the new external professional only stayed for three months. By June 1988, Odair informally managed the entire technology area and became the de facto boss. In January 1989, the third generation of a family from the Northeast took charge of information technology at Nitro Química. Similar to other factory managers, Odair was tasked with outsourcing. Information technology was not the primary focus of Nitro Química, similar to manufacturing wooden spoons and soccer cleats. Consequently, information technology also adopted the philosophy of outsourcing.

Odair's office overlooked Ricardo Ermírio de Moraes' office in the adjacent building, where the board of directors was located. Odair's building was situated in the center among the new factories, in the same building where rayon production had started in the 1930s. They named the first building the Data Processing Center (DPC) or simply DPC when the new buildings were constructed.

In February, shortly after assuming his position officially, Odair presented his plan for the IT area to Ricardo. During the meeting, Odair discussed outsourcing and how it would benefit Nitro Química. Ricardo agreed with the plan, recognizing the importance of focusing on the core business, even if it wasn't obvious at the time. Odair was tasked with figuring out how to implement outsourcing in his area.

However, the technicians in the DPC building had different opinions. They believed that managing the employees' sense of loss would be challenging, despite the potential increase in business focus and profitability through outsourcing. Arguing solely about profitability felt cold and of little value to them. Paradoxically, outsourcing would be detrimental even to those who claimed to take pride in working at Nitro Química. The company held a sacred status. But since when did sacred things have to yield profits? In that year of 1990, many employees completed 30 or 40 years of service at Nitro Química.

When Odair began planning the outsourcing process, he supervised a team of 88 people in the IT department. Some criticized his actions, claiming he didn't know what he was doing and that the idea would fail. In response, Odair stated that Nitro Química's primary focus was not information technology.

Another obstacle was that São Miguel Paulista was not located in the IT company hubs on Avenida Paulista or Avenida Brigadeiro Faria Lima. It was time-consuming and costly for employees of those companies to commute to kilometer 26 of Rodovia dos Trabalhadores. Nitro Química trained its professionals, but due to the closed market and IBM's proprietary systems, they often left for other opportunities. The market would attract them, resulting in a significant loss of employees for Odair.

All these challenges made outsourcing a difficult task to carry out. For two years, Odair listened to the professionals in the DPC building who doubted the feasibility of outsourcing. Meanwhile, he researched companies in the market, always in search of the best service provider. Instead of following the usual approach of creating an in-house or mixed IT solution, such as Villares partnering with IBM or Banco Itaú establishing Itautec, Odair and Ricardo sought a completely independent alternative for Nitro Química.

It was a complex undertaking. IT providers were still unprofessional, partly due to the information technology reserve. Various outsourcing models were tested, but the services were often costly and did not consistently meet the required quality standards.

While Odair searched for a reliable service provider, Marco faced a personal crisis caused by Collor's seizure. He needed a stable income for Stefanini, as the revenue from training programs was too unpredictable to sustain the company.

Stefanini found itself at a turning point, reaching the first curve. According to the next curve theory, entrepreneurs often fail because they fail to strategically adapt after starting their venture. They set rigid goals and become part of the statistics of businesses that shut down within the first two years. The theory emphasizes the importance of being flexible, as it is impossible to predict the future beyond the initial years. Entrepreneurs should focus on short-term predictions and remain open to business opportunities while being aware of potential challenges such as economic crises, technological changes, or misjudgments of the market.

At that moment, Marco was approaching that curve with Stefanini. He realized that relying solely on lessons and training programs wouldn't be enough for the company's survival. The scope needed to be expanded. During his search for technicians and managers for his courses, Marco met Odair, which presented an opportunity.

This opportunity led to a pilgrimage of sorts, with Marco traveling endlessly between Avenida Paulista and São Miguel Paulista. Unlike the training programs where he could take the bus, he had to rely on borrowing Milton's Saveiro pickup truck, which he eventually ended up keeping. He would travel the approximately 30 kilometers between Stefanini and the Nitro Química factory.

During these travels, Marco visited the Data Processing Center (DPC) and found a familiar environment with a mainframe and an information system called CICS (Custom Information Control System). This was nothing out of the ordinary for him. He returned to make his pitch, had meetings with Odair, managers, and executives, all while studying the company's mainframe usage.

Through these interactions, Marco discovered the missing piece. Nitro Química's IT department needed well-defined and efficient processes to carry out their tasks. Every time a system access terminal was placed or relocated, a software analyst had to reconfigure CICS and restart the mainframe and terminals. The same applied to printing machines. In essence, the company experienced frequent interruptions.

System shutdowns would also occur, impacting activities like billing, finance, and supplies. Some users claimed to be unable to access the systems multiple times a week. The next system shutdown was unpredictable and would happen three or four times a week.

Marco recognized that this problem was not exclusive to Nitro Química. Even banks would have 50 branches go offline simply based on instructions from tech support. Odair could only address this issue by partnering with a supplier who could deliver quality services. After nearly ten trips to São Miguel, Marco succeeded and secured his first outsourcing contract.

With Marco's involvement, Odair established processes to address the pressing issues. The immediate focus was to eliminate surprise system shutdowns by implementing planned procedures, even during the late hours of the night. Marco began planning capacity and analyzing the performance of the IT infrastructure, just as he did for Bradesco. He visited São Miguel Paulista three times a week and spent at least part of his time there.

However, the key aspect of the contract was the outsourcing of technical support. This required Stefanini to provide personnel to be stationed at the Nitro Química factory. Since Stefanini's focus was information technology, they had a vast pool of professionals to draw from in their portfolio. Those who accepted the positions at Nitro Química knew that they would have the opportunity to work at São Miguel Paulista for a few years, but they also saw the potential for growth in a company focused on the technology sector. Odair hired four permanent staff members to handle the factory's technical support, as well as three or four occasional workers to address any additional needs. One of the new hires was specifically responsible for online application processing and had expertise in CICS.

Despite the initial skepticism from colleagues who believed outsourcing technical support wouldn't work, Odair persisted with his decision. There were some unscheduled shutdowns in the first and second months after the new team started working, but by the third month, the work routine at Nitro Química experienced no interruptions. Technical support became so seamless that everyone forgot it was outsourced.

Outsourcing brought significant benefits but also brought changes to Nitro Química, a company that had initially arrived in Brazil by sea. Out of the 5,000 employees hired when Ricardo took over, Nitro Química ended up with only 800. However, the company achieved a substantial gain in productivity.

For Marco Stefanini, outsourcing was confirmed as the right path. More contracts, including one with Johnson & Johnson, were yet to come. In 1990, lectures earned Stefanini USD 100,000. However, with the new contracts in 1991, the company's revenue soared to USD 700,000. Although the profitability was lower compared to training programs, the work became less seasonal with more guarantees. In 1991, Stefanini moved from their small office on Avenida Paulista to a space four times larger on Avenida Faria Lima. They occupied 260 square meters in the renowned Cal Center building.

In 1991, a change occurred in the market, including within Nitro Química. Odair proposed another daring plan for the company's management, which ultimately led to Stefanini losing the Nitro Química contract the following year, along with many other contracts.

CHAPTER 6

SHRINKAGE

O ut of the corner of his eye, Marco observed the box, estimating its height to be no higher than his waistline. Intrigued, he approached it for a closer look. With two fingers, he gently pushed the box aside, finding it surprisingly light, confirming his initial assumption. This black box represented the popular desktop computer that had been gaining traction and was posing a threat to Stefanini's business.

Although it wasn't the first time Marco had encountered a desktop computer, he still had limited knowledge about these machines. His expertise and focus revolved around mainframes, whether they were Unix-based, minicomputers, or even PCs used as servers. Mainframes had been his world for more than seven years since he first encountered them at Bradesco in 1984. He vividly remembered the sight of two tapes spinning inside a blue and beige box, resembling a small closet or a washing machine. He firmly believed in the indispensability of large, powerful mainframes for major companies. However, as the early 1990s approached, even the staunchest supporters of big computers were starting to question their future relevance, although they might not openly admit it to others.

The economic environment made entrepreneurs skittish, as usual in Brazil. The previous year's inflation had exploded at a rate of 1,476%. In the United States, interest rates were slowly starting to descend, but the impact would take time to be felt in Brazil.

Was that a problem at the time? Maybe not. However, it helps to keep in mind a fundamental part of the business flow of IT services: always work one year ahead. If you are not selling anything now, you won't have much to do next year.

Marco started to enter outsourcing contracts in 1990, and this new offering resulted in a broken record in the following year. But while Stefanini worked and made a profit in 1991, the course of business indicated a very poor 1992. Throughout 1991, Marco had heard of companies planning to shift away from mainframes. Relevant migrations from mainframes to desktops were carried out that year. The migration was referred to as downsizing.

Originally, the name had nothing to do with information technology. Downsizing had several meanings, perhaps originally appearing in the 1970s. While Milton Stefanini still believed in Brazil, the oil crisis hit Americans hard, since they were paying more than they were used to for fuel. It made more sense to have smaller cars and houses, a less expensive way of life. That was downsizing for US consumers. Less is more – a philosophy that started inside people's homes.

It was only in the following decade that the term would invade companies and end up shrinking the careers of many. North American and later European and Japanese companies ordered layoffs in droves. Less is more worked even better when it came to profits.

The economic crisis was not the only element that would stimulate layoffs. Computers were multiplying and often reduced the need for humans carrying out tasks. From 1980 through 1995, at least 13 million Americans were fired from their jobs. Some estimates around 39 million workers thrown to the curb.

Most of these layoffs ended up being concentrated in the 1990s, known as the decade of downsizing. Between 1992 and 1997 alone, over 16 million American workers lost their jobs. They were being "downsized." In many cases, all of this could just have been a euphemism for being fired, but management gurus have tried to turn that problem into a good thing. Crises can be beneficial.

The fad arrived in Brazil before long. Here, just as it was abroad, the goal was to eliminate unnecessary corporate bureaucracy, gain efficiencies and increase profits. When carried out correctly, the process entailed having executive think about how to restructure in line with the business plan before sending people away. There were catastrophes and triumphs; ultimately, however, downsizing was making businesses leaner.

When DPCs started to switch from mainframes to PCs or minicomputers for servers, it was only natural that the same term would be used. First, they shrunk the way of life, then jobs. Now was the time to shrink computers! And downsizing made big waves in the technology market worldwide.

For Marco, it was as if the choice he had made in 1984, when he joined Bradesco, was now being challenged. That same year, the federal government had imposed a reserve on information technology in Brazil. The law was becoming seven years old and was to be eliminated in the following year. With new technologies coming, there were new rules, a new world. Smaller, no doubt, for businesses; perhaps even for Marco.

In Brazil, downsizing was all the rage in businesses and IT departments. This was also true at Nitro Química. It made perfect sense, as downsizing was supposed to increase efficiency and profit as much as outsourcing. In the same year that Marco did well by closing the contract, Odair approved a proposal to hire the Arthur Andersen consulting firm. The consultancy was to evaluate the possibility of abandoning the mainframe.

Odair wanted to downsize even before meeting Stefanini, since 1989, prior to taking over the company's IT area. In 1991, already the IT director, Odair needed to show more results. Despite the success of the service outsourcing process, executives at Nitro Química wanted to keep cutting; in order to do so, they planned to terminate the contract with IBM and its large computers.

Downsizing involved, after migrating, keeping the two platforms co-existing and working for a period. This was a point in Stefanini's favor, who could enter yet another deal (Odair himself believed that Marco would be able to serve them). However, the balance tipped towards Arthur Andersen, which had a sound brand in the market and had already been hired to assess the impact of downsizing at Nitro Química. And it was Arthur Andersen that actually ended up getting the contract. Soon after, the North American consultancy was also chosen by Nitro Química to provide technical support services, the same line of work that had given Stefanini so much work and pride. People do say that bad news come in droves.

Later, however, Odair discovered that Arthur Andersen didn't have that much experience shrinking computers either, and all of them had to learn together. All this trailblazing came at a cost: the budget of USD 2.5 million dollars in 10 months broke – officially – at USD 250,000.

Even with higher spending, companies continued to downsize; in reaction to the predicted and imminent end of the IT reserve, they were poised to seize the moment by exchanging the mainframe for smaller, more efficient and cheaper pieces of equipment. Technicians operating with languages such as Visual Basic (VB) and Delphi set up small companies, offering services focused on the new environment. Stefanini was still completely based on the technical knowledge provided by Marco, who, after the first systems, had barely any contact with PCs. The growth of Microland and other alternatives to the mainframe was a direct blow to Stefanini, which made its money exclusively by operating and giving training on mainframes.

This meant Marco was losing twice with downsizing. There were fewer mainframe systems to operate, and therefore fewer outsourcing contracts like the one they earned – and lost – with Nitro Química. And he was also left out of contracts for migration to desktops simply because he didn't know PCs well, much less minicomputers or Unix systems. For a young and ambitious company, it felt like the beginning of the end before it even took off.

For Marco, downsizing was even worse than the Collor hijacking. With that turn in the market, he would face a crisis in which he would not be able to grow. This experience taught Marco that heavily relying on one company or technology was too dangerous. Marco needed to diversify and, above all, enter the world of the desktops posthaste.

All he needed was a client. In the services market, there is a clear strategic dilemma. Every client always asks if the supplier has experience in the service offered. If they don't, it's very difficult to get customers. For new companies without a consolidated brand in other markets, it is almost impossible. Hence, the vicious circle that drives away new businesses.

The case of Odair and Nitro Química was precisely that. Arthur Andersen was already in-house, had international renown and demonstrated its expertise in planning the downsizing process. Marco needed to jump that hurdle.

The first step was to find someone with experience. And, once again, a colleague from Bradesco entered Stefanini's story.

Electronic engineer Luiz Edmundo took the same course that led Marco to the world of information technology in 1984. It was he who pretty much tied with Marco in the final grade ranking. He worked at Bradesco for three and a half years before moving on to American Express. From there, he went on to work at the University of Marília and then at Informatel, a services bureau of Grupo Vicunha, where he had his first experience with downsizing.

In 1991, Marco called Luiz Edmundo to provide consulting work for Stefanini. With him, it was already possible to say that they had in-house experience with downsizing. Now, all they needed was a client.

For months, Marco's conversations with potential clients also included downsizing-related projects. Nothing came out of that, however. On that afternoon in August 1991, yet another Friday with intense traffic in São Paulo, Marco left a client and headed for Rodovia dos Trabalhadores (three years later, it would be renamed Rodovia Ayrton Senna). It was the way to get to the headquarters of a tractor company based in Mogi das Cruzes, Valtra, then named Valmet. In the passenger's seat, he carried a six-page envelope: it was a proposal with a plan for Valmet's upcoming downsizing.

Originally, Valmet was a Finnish state-owned company, created in 1951 from factories used during the Second World War. It established its only factory outside Finland in Brazil in 1960, a situation that continues to this day. This move allowed Valmet to capture 30% of the Brazilian tractor market and utilize its production for exports to 60 countries.

In the early 1990s, Valmet was a significant company with computer infrastructure that surpassed its needs. Like most Brazilian companies at that time, Valmet utilized a mainframe, which remained mostly idle. Roberto Massucci, who headed the

IT department, had a different background compared to Luiz Edmundo. Roberto joined Bradesco at the age of 14 and attended a technically-focused high school program. He learned the IT trade and worked at various companies such as Eucatex, Honda, and Light. In the midst of the 1984 economic crisis, Roberto decided to leave the bustling city of São Paulo and moved to Mogi das Cruzes to join Valmet, while Luiz Edmundo and Marco took a different path by staying at the bank.

After nearly seven years at Valmet, Roberto became responsible for the company's IT area. However, there was limited room for investment as most of the technology budget was allocated to maintaining the infrastructure, particularly the mainframe. In response to a request from the company's president to reduce expenses, Roberto and the president recognized that downsizing servers would be the simplest solution. However, they acknowledged that an in-house assessment would be inadequate due to the department's lack of technical expertise. Stefanini, an external company, was still attempting to enter into a partnership with Valmet.

Despite Stefanini's lack of downsizing experience, Roberto met with Marco and found the idea of hiring a company without preconceived notions appealing. He sought an independent assessment and preferred alternatives to more experienced companies that came with closed software partnerships. Marco, aware of the risks of relying on a single technology for business, decided to offer an unbiased assessment. Less than three months later, in August 1991, Marco secured his first service contract related to downsizing.

At that point, the task involved planning the migration, specifically downsizing the mainframe to desktops. It was not only a good opportunity but also provided valuable experience and the prospect of executing the downsizing process. Starting in October, Marco made regular trips of 70 kilometers along Rodovia dos Trabalhadores and spent a significant part of his day at the company. On his first day of work, he parked his car near the building where the company's restaurant was located and descended the staircase. The Data Processing Center (DPC) was situated downstairs, despite being on the ground floor on the opposite side of the building due to the slope. Marco entered the room where Roberto was waiting – that was the DPC.

The room, measuring 225 square meters, housed the IBM 4381 mainframe, which occupied slightly over a third of the space. Marco didn't need to closely examine it; he was familiar with its operation. There were several cabinets, and the entire setup weighed several tonnes. This powerful machine would be replaced by a few small servers, portable enough for anyone to carry. Times had indeed changed.

Roberto then took Marco to the adjacent building, where the president's office was located. The president discussed the type of technological infrastructure that Valmet should have, marking the beginning of their ongoing conversations. Over the next four months, Marco traveled along Rodovia dos Trabalhadores to meet with the two executives, as well as several others from the human resources and finance departments. Upon returning to Stefanini's office in São Paulo, Marco would sit down with Luiz Edmundo and provide him with a detailed breakdown. They thoroughly examined the company's needs and evaluated the potential capabilities of running systems on servers that were less powerful than a mainframe. By January 1992, the planning phase was complete.

Marco presented an enticing proposition to Valmet's president, suggesting that significant cost savings could be achieved by transitioning from the mainframe to desktop computers. The plan involved replacing the large IBM mainframe with three smaller servers: a larger one for manufacturing, a medium-sized one for marketing and sales, and a small one for human resources. This shift would not only reduce machine costs but also cut down on air conditioning expenses. The executives were impressed with the proposal, and Marco anticipated winning another contract. However, he was not successful this time.

Roberto, believing that the Valmet team had sufficient expertise compared to other market players, decided that they could handle the downsizing process themselves. He successfully convinced the board of this approach. The infrastructure in Mogi das Cruzes was substantial, with nearly 200 dumb terminals connected to the mainframe and a network of coaxial cables spanning the entire company. Valmet's Finnish headquarters had already shown positive reactions to the downsizing project.

Aware of their significant relationship with IBM, Roberto contacted the company as soon as he received Stefanini's planning. He hoped to receive a counter-proposal or, at the very least, convince IBM to reconsider the existing contract that tied Valmet to the mainframe. Initially, IBM indicated it would be difficult to disregard the contract and allow Valmet to abandon mainframes sooner.

To address the situation, Roberto personally visited IBM's renowned building on Rua Tutoia, holding several meetings. In the final meeting, Valmet's account manager at IBM remained steadfast. Roberto felt he had exhausted his alternatives and, expressing his intention to carry out the downsizing and end the commitment, abruptly stood up from his chair. Realizing they were about to lose a client, possibly for a long time, the IBM employee insisted that Roberto sit down to continue the conversation.

Eventually, Valmet was offered a substantial discount by IBM. Monthly expenses related to the mainframe would decrease by over 50%. Additionally, Valmet committed to purchasing $1 million worth of products and services from IBM within two years. This expense transformed into an investment, with 100% of the servers, desktops, and laptops at Valmet becoming IBM products. The investment included a new network with structured cabling, costing $450,000, consisting of four kilometers of optical fiber connecting ten buildings with 400 network points. This network became the first of its kind in Brazil, and Roberto received visits from other companies interested in witnessing this cutting-edge infrastructure. The mainframe would continue to serve Valmet for another ten years.

Roberto's tough negotiation with IBM exemplifies the changes occurring in the market at that time. IBM couldn't provide discounts to every company at any given time, and many companies ultimately opted for downsizing. Stefanini's consultancy for Valmet Tratores was pivotal as it marked their first portfolio outside of mainframes.

The service carried out in 1992 by Marco sparked a reaction, but overcoming the threat would still require time. Downsizing proved to be more challenging than the hijacking carried out by the Collor administration. In fact, 1992 was the only year in which Stefanini's revenues were lower than the previous year, dipping from $700,000 in 1991 to $500,000. This experience taught Marco the importance of not relying solely on one company or technology. Depending too heavily on a single entity could lead to initial gains when the technology is adopted and customers show interest, but when that technology becomes obsolete, the company suffers.

In 1992, Luiz Edmundo, then 32 years old, was hired to handle downsizing projects. Marco offered him a fixed salary and the possibility of variable earnings, which was uncommon in the market. It was at this point that Luiz Edmundo secured the contract to oversee the downsizing of Refinações de Milho Brasil, involving the migration from JD Edwards management software to an AS400 server.

Following the successful migrations, Stefanini's focus shifted towards technical support contracts in the desktop realm, contrasting with the previous emphasis on code development in the mainframe world. The advice provided to Valmet played a crucial role in expanding Stefanini's services into a new area, marking a transition from a one-person venture to a company offering a wider range of services. As a result, Marco's role evolved from execution to management.

With the establishment of the new services division and the recovery of the market, Stefanini's revenues experienced significant growth. By the end of 1993, the company's revenues reached $1 million, and the following year, it soared to $3 million. The achievements fueled a sense of accomplishment, leading to the relocation of Stefanini's headquarters from the 8th floor in Faria Lima to a larger space on the 12th floor, effectively doubling their office size. From its humble beginnings with 40 employees and a cramped office on Avenida Paulista, Stefanini now boasted over 100 employees serving various clients.

In early 1995, Luiz Edmundo made a wager with Marco, predicting that their annual sales would reach $10 million. At that time, they couldn't anticipate the events that would unfold in the subsequent months. In response, Marco expressed a more realistic view, suggesting that reaching $4 million would be feasible, but he also added a touch of skepticism, urging Luiz Edmundo to be realistic in their expectations.

CHAPTER 7

THE TEQUILA EFFECT

The atmosphere was tense on that Saturday afternoon, March 23, 1994, as a crowd anxiously surrounded Mexican candidate Luis Donaldo Colosio Murrieta. Unbeknownst to him, a revolver was brought to his forehead, and a single bullet pierced through. Murrieta fell, and the crisis that followed was profound.

This assassination set in motion a chain of events that would lead to one of the most staggering economic hurricanes in history. Just three months earlier, the Zapatista army had initiated a war in the state of Chiapas, further adding to the instability. International investors grew increasingly hesitant to invest in a country with a struggling economy teetering on the edge of civil war. The slightest misstep could cause Mexico to collapse.

To fill the void left by Murrieta's assassination, President Salinas selected Ernesto Zedillo, who had been involved in the campaign. Zedillo would go on to win the election in August, temporarily easing concerns in the markets. However, the subsequent rise in interest rates further exacerbated the state of the Mexican economy. In November 1994, the United States raised its interest rates by 0.75%, prompting billions of dollars to flee Mexico in favor of its more stable neighbor. The crisis deepened.

Amidst these tumultuous circumstances, Marco recognized the need to expand Stefanini. The opening of the Brazilian IT market had attracted the attention of multinational companies, and domestic competitors were rapidly growing through partnerships. Having experienced the downsizing crisis alongside IBM, Marco remained cautious about relying too heavily on a single technology or partnership. Furthermore, he understood the risks associated with depending solely on one market. The city of São Paulo, where Stefanini was based, was gradually becoming too limiting for the company's ambitions.

The first step toward expansion occurred almost serendipitously, driven by the changing dynamics of the market.

During 1994, an important person in Stefanini's history also needed to set a new professional direction. The young man in question was Márcio Da Mata, who was neither a technician nor had graduated in anything related to the exact sciences. In 1988, he left college with a degree in business administration.

At the time, he worked at the São Paulo State Basic Sanitation Company (Sabesp), where he would stay for ten years; however, the state-owned company dealt in engineering, and he knew that information technology was just the means of making its processes more efficient. Márcio thought that this was a limit to his growth. That was when Stefanini's invitation came.

Long before leaving Sabesp, Márcio had already worked for the training and IT services company. Throughout 1993, three or four nights a week, he would go give classes on Oracle at Stefanini's office on Avenida Faria Lima, in the Cal Center Building – something he was very fond of. But in 1994, while the crisis in Mexico worsened and Zedillo began to deal with an unstable country, Stefanini's courses in Brazil were less in demand, as we have seen. And just as Márcio felt it was time to actually think about a change in his professional life, Marco also felt the need to expand his course options.

So, Marco invited Márcio to work at Stefanini in a permanent capacity. The invitation was accepted, of course. Márcio left

Sabesp and started working at Stefanini full time. He started doing background work as a technical consultant, serving companies like Caterpillar, Paulista Seguros, and Editora Abril. However, he truly wanted more. He just needed to wait for the right time.

Despite the lack of courses and uncertainties, there was a sense of confidence in the air – both at Stefanini and in Brazil. Unlike our turbulent sombrero-wearing neighbor in North America, expectations in Brazil were even more positive due to the start of the Real Plan, created just 24 days before Mexico's Murrieta was shot in the temple.

Time passed... All Brazilians were rooting for the Real Plan to succeed, while in Mexico there was an intense dread over an ever-approaching crisis. Five days before Christmas, the fuse that had been lit with Murrieta's murder came to an end and the bomb exploded. Zedillo was forced to abandon the peso-dollar parity and to adopt the floating exchange rate model. Almost immediately, the dollar doubled in value. Thousands of companies went bankrupt, unemployment soared, half the value of the Mexican stock market evaporated and capital fled the country. The crisis ultimately spread throughout the world, especially in Latin America, causing the "Tequila Effect."

The first victim was Argentina. In the first two months of 1995, six small banks were subject to intervention from the country's Central Bank. At the end of the year, 40 Argentinean banks or non-bank institutions shut down.

In Brazil, the Stock Exchange lost 35% of its value in three weeks, and all gains accumulated with the Real Plan were lost. In March, to solve the financial hangover, the Brazilian government raised interest rates and now had the highest rates in real terms globally (30%).

While the economic world was reeling from the tequila, the scenario was even more demanding for Brazilian banks, which had also lost revenue with the dip in inflation after the Real Plan. Previously, they took 20% of their revenue from the financial circus. After the Real Plan, the same activities would bring only 1%. One of those banks that needed to reinvent itself was Bamerindus, and its executives were looking for ways to reduce administrative costs. One of these courses of action was precisely to make the IT infrastructure cheaper. The old adage repeated itself and, once again, a moment of crisis led to opportunities.

The way to make infrastructure cheaper was to, once again, downsize the mainframe. To carry out the downsizing, Bamerindus hired the technology multinational HP, which spent the year of 1994 looking for partners to help with the work (in a process known as "quarteirizar" in the Brazilian market – passing on the service in whole or in part after winning an outsourcing contract). In early 1995, Marco saw HP as a good business partner and discussed the opportunity with his employees. One of them stood up and asked to work on that project. That was Márcio Da Mata.

Someone had to do the job, and Marco agreed that it should be Márcio. The young technician had no idea how important that HP project would be in the future. The leadership and all the hiring of the staff that would downsize the Bamerindus mainframe were thus under Márcio's responsibility.

Stefanini, however, was a year late in the competition for the project. Other companies providing IT services had already been trying to reach an agreement with HP for months, but the first major hurdle was getting qualified people to work. The project was immense and complex: Bamerindus intended to simply deactivate its mainframe and move all applications and systems to the desktop. With a leaner infrastructure, the cost would decrease, and thus the institution could face the difficulties imposed by the Tequila Effect while losing less money.

At that time, Stefanini finally had proven experience with downsizing, but a project like Banco Bamerindus seemed too grandiose. There were nearly 1,500 branches, all of them pioneers in the use of microcomputers in Brazil, which greatly expedited the service it provided to its two million account holders. Stefanini's challenge was to tinker with that huge technological infrastructure and turn everything upside down. Márcio was unaware of the size of the project, but he didn't let discouragement overwhelm him.

The day after the conversation with Marco, he started searching for his team. He needed people who knew object-oriented programming and the C++ language. USP and Unicamp were the only places where one could find experts in these areas. However, Márcio considered these college experts to be too "academic." In layman's terms: people who rarely left the classroom and had never faced a big project, much less something as gigantic as the one Stefanini was going to carry out.

Márcio decided to go straight to the market in search of people who truly knew those technologies. He placed advertisements in newspapers like Estadão and asked around if anyone knew good professionals. When he got a lead, it was truly difficult to get to talk to the person. In the pre-mobile phone days, the only way to find the professional was to call the person at home at night (they couldn't talk freely about job invitations in their current workplace).

At night, when he was home, he would sit on the couch and start making the phone calls. Márcio lived in a shared residence with friends, who complained about how much he would use the phone – sometimes it went on for hours. With mocking smiles, they would shout from their rooms: "Get off the phone, Márcio, all you do is call your girlfriends!"

Months went by, and all that effort barely yielded any results. Márcio then decided to go back to the academic world. One night, he went looking for the graduating class of the computer science course at USP. He arrived just before the break and waited by the door. The first student left, but Márcio did not approach him.

"He looks like a teenager, no dice," he thought.

Another came out; he was wearing slippers. Better luck with the next one.

The third student came by. Márcio took a step forward and said bluntly:

Do you know object-oriented programming?

By the end of the night, he had hired two professionals. It was June 1995, almost four months after the talent hunt began.

He asked for other indications from the first two. He continued to make calls from home during weeknights, sometimes as late as 11 pm or on Sundays. Ultimately, he hired 25 professionals from USP. Within three months, Stefanini had become one of the two main suppliers for HP's Bamerindus project (there were at least a dozen companies providing this type of service). At that time, Márcio's group boasted 40 professionals in total.

It was a major challenge. In order to downsize the mainframe and write the new systems, the Stefanini team needed to understand the old systems from top to bottom. For that, working remotely just wouldn't cut it – everyone had to go to Paraná, to the bank's headquarters. Marco Stefanini was fully booking the small twin-engine turbo-prop plane of Linhas Aéreas Pantanal (acquired by TAM at the end of 2009), which could fit 50 people.

The group convened on Sunday evenings at Congonhas Airport. They all boarded the biplane and disembarked at the old Bacacheri airport in Curitiba. Throughout the week, they engaged in discussions with various departments, conducted meetings, and worked on drafting specifications and code. Some team members were even sent to India, where they collaborated with another HP partner to receive processed information and write code for the new systems. This occurrence in 1995 exemplified how Indian companies were ahead of Brazilian counterparts in exporting services.

The codes were subsequently delivered to Brazil, and the Stefanini team took on the responsibility of implementing each component of the project. This task was complex and occasionally stressful, as the Brazilians had to revise many portions due to the Indians' limited understanding of the bank's business rules. Although the Indians excelled at coding, their youth and lack of experience remained evident. Unfortunately, this situation has not changed significantly, as many outsourcing projects in India today still encounter similar issues.

This routine persisted for a year, with Márcio and a significant portion of the team flying back and forth to Curitiba every week. Meanwhile, the partnership with HP extended beyond Bamerindus. Almost simultaneously, contracts with Nacional, Finasa, and Alcatel were secured. However, once all these projects were underway, Marco realized that nearly a third of his revenue relied exclusively on the HP partnership. This posed a risky situation where any misstep could have dire consequences. And indeed, something went wrong.

A premonition of trouble emerged on Friday, August 25, 1995. A portion of Stefanini's funds was invested in Banco Irmãos Guimarães, commonly known as BIG. Marco and Graça grew concerned about keeping their money there and contemplated transferring it elsewhere, possibly to British Lloyds banks. Following lunch, Graça dialed the bank, determined to redeem her investment. However, either they did not answer or the line was engaged. She spent the entire afternoon attempting to reach them. It happened to be the anniversary of the investment, and the Stefanini couple were waiting for this milestone to transfer their investment to the British bank, considering it a safer option after the bankruptcy of Banco Econômico, a major bank in England.

As the day drew to a close, with 6:30 pm already past, everyone had already left Stefanini. Marco remained at his desk, working, while Graça closed the door to her office on the 12th floor of the Cal Center Building. But before leaving, she stopped by the front desk and made one final attempt to contact the bank. This time, they picked up.

"Phew!" exclaimed Graça. "I've been trying to reach you all afternoon."

On the other end, a voice responded with words that left Graça speechless for several seconds. She hung up the phone and hurried across the company to find her husband.

"Marco, BIG has been liquidated," she gasped, slightly breathless. "I think we've lost everything!"

The loss of money was substantial, but Stefanini had secured other contracts, leading Marco to believe they could swiftly recover. However, two months later, he discovered that the downfall of BIG was only the beginning of their troubles.

On a late afternoon in Brasília, Saturday, November 3, 1995, the lights illuminated one of the upper floors of the Central Bank building as board members continued their meeting, which aimed to establish Proer. Though it was merely a nickname, the full name of the program was more revealing - the Program to Stimulate the Restructuring and Strengthening of the National

Financial System. In essence, this initiative aimed to fill the gap left by yet another financial crisis, and Proer utilized public funds to achieve this.

Brazil was grappling with the aftermath of the Tequila Effect, and Marco, along with everyone at Stefanini, was about to face a major challenge. The issue that originated with a murder in Mexico would soon impact the contracts they had secured with HP. The first casualty would be the partnership with Banco Nacional, one of Brazil's largest banks, known for its sponsorship of the late Ayrton Senna, the Formula One driver who had passed away the previous year.

Precisely at that moment, Marco finalized the staffing requirements for the bank project. In terms of the number of Stefanini professionals involved, Nacional already surpassed other important clients such as Refinações de Milho Brasil, which had seven personnel, and Chase Manhattan, which had ten. The Nacional project necessitated the collaboration of 30 professionals, a result of Marco's arduous efforts over several months.

During the same weekend that Proer was being drafted, Unibanco executives received a call from the Central Bank, requesting their evaluation of Nacional. Two weeks after Proer was announced, the federal government issued an Interim Measure that enabled the closure of the institution's financial hole and the forced sale of the company to Unibanco. The deal was finalized on Friday, November 17. News of the decisions made at the Central Bank building made headlines over the weekend. Márcio watched the developments on TV and called Marco.

"What do we do now?" Márcio asked.

Marco's response was simple: "We'll see on Monday."

Naturally, the loss of such a significant contract was a cause for concern. However, Marco's first priority was to decide how to handle his employees. They still had one month of work remaining, but after that, Nacional would no longer be paying for their services. Knowing the effort it took to find and recruit these professionals, Marco believed it would be a mistake to let them leave Stefanini.

Consequently, everyone mobilized to reassign the team to other clients. Marco personally accompanied one or more professionals on visits to clients, highlighting the outstanding work they had done for a major Brazilian bank. This approach was successful in 95% of cases. Those who wished to stay at Stefanini were able to do so.

Meanwhile, Márcio continued traveling to Curitiba to oversee the Bamerindus project. This contract was even larger than Nacional, involving 40 personnel from Stefanini. However, months after the collapse of Nacional, Bamerindus also started experiencing financial difficulties. It was the year 1996.

This wasn't the first time Bamerindus faced such challenges. Nearly a decade earlier, in 1986, the British bank Midland, one of Bamerindus' shareholders, had sent a large sum of dollars by plane to save the struggling Paraná bank. In the following years, Bamerindus managed to turn things around and introduced innovative products like the remunerated account. The number of branches increased from 600 to over 1,500.

However, with Midland being acquired by HSBC, the world's largest bank now had concerns about the fate of Bamerindus, in which it held a stake. Time passed, but Bamerindus' situation showed little improvement. In mid-March 1997, another plane arrived, this time with executives who came to study local regulations, select desirable assets, and do what was inevitable: fully acquire Bamerindus.

The total sale to HSBC, worth USD 1 billion, was reported to the Central Bank. In the late afternoon of March 26, 1997, after the market closed, the Central Bank decreed an intervention, serving as a transitional phase in the sale to HSBC. With a new owner came new standards, technologies, and systems. Some ongoing projects were allowed to continue, but many were eventually suspended or canceled.

Márcio completed his work in Curitiba and returned to São Paulo four months after the intervention. Stefanini lost its final and largest contract in the partnership with HP, which had accounted for 30% of the company's revenue.

Without the Bamerindus contract, another successful effort was made to reassign employees. Despite the setback, Stefanini's consolidation was assured. The projects undertaken with Nacional and, particularly, Bamerindus had positioned Stefanini strongly in the financial market. At that time, the company had a unique offering: professionals experienced in both desktop servers and the financial sector.

Furthermore, Marco had expanded beyond São Paulo and established the first branch in Paraná. Later on, HSBC would become a recurring customer of Stefanini. However, during that period, Marco had returned to São Paulo, and his earnings were affected by the loss of the Bamerindus contract.

The expansion into Paraná had been made possible by a significant contract, contributing to Stefanini's financial performance. The geographical and financial growth didn't stop with Bamerindus, though. While Márcio Da Mata was searching for more personnel to send to Curitiba, another Stefanini employee was embarking on a personal journey outside São Paulo, all within the troubled year of 1995.

CHAPTER 8

COUNTRYSIDE

T he D-20 truck was cruising towards Campinas. The cloudy sky made Bruno Mondin step on the gas. The road was still dry, even though it rained relentlessly in the last weeks of that warm winter of 1995 (it would be the rainiest in the next fifteen years). He wanted to arrive in Campinas before six in the afternoon. In the back of the truck, Bruno carried a table, three chairs, and a telephone: furniture for Stefanini's new office outside the city of São Paulo.

Since he was a child, going from city to city had become routine for Bruno. His father was a construction engineer, and whenever he needed to travel for a new job, he took his family across the country in tow. When Bruno was born, his father was working in the West of São Paulo, which meant the boy became a native of Presidente Prudente. From there, the family moved 200 kilometers east when the father started working at the Promissão Hydroelectric Power Plant. Bruno would live part of his childhood in Campinas but would still travel a lot, passing through Lins, Rio de Janeiro, Petrópolis, Santos, São Bernardo do Campo, and many other places.

All that traveling had a reason: Bruno's father worked at Cetenco Engenharia, an 80-year-old contractor that became as big as Camargo Correa and Andrade Gutierrez. Therefore, wherever there was an important worksite, the Mondin family was there. In addition to the hydroelectric plant built when Bruno was born, he also lived close to the construction of works such as the Bandeirantes Highway, the Imigrantes Highway, and the Paulo Afonso Hydroelectric Power Plant. Traveling had always been part of the Mondins' life.

As a teenager, Bruno studied computing at the Piracicaba School of Engineering. As a freshman, he got his first job at Caterpillar, and there he met Marco Stefanini, who gave lectures there. Shortly before graduating, at the age of 21, he accepted Marco's invitation and went to work in Stefanini's pre-sales area (he basically wrote commercial proposals and provided technical support). He stayed on the job for two years. In early 1995, Bruno received a second proposal from Marco. This time, it felt tailor-made for him.

It was at the end of the workday, on a hot afternoon in the São Paulo summer. Everyone went down for drinks at the foot of the Cal Center Building. Marco, as always, talked about work even over a beer. At that time, he was particularly excited about the contracts won in the partnership with HP. There were many opportunities across Brazil, and Marco didn't want to wait for the phone to ring. Stefanini needed to leave São Paulo by itself.

Two other IT companies tried to set up branches in the São Paulo countryside, without much success. At the time, the West of São Paulo did not have major companies (unlike today, with large slaughterhouses and plants). However, in the rest of the São Paulo countryside, there were many national and global companies, with several interesting prospects, such as the two contracts that Stefanini had already secured up to that moment: Caterpillar, where Marco had met Bruno, and Magazine Luiza. Both contracts provided but a small taste of what could be achieved. Between sips of beer, Marco asked Bruno if he would be willing to go back to the region that he knew so well.

Marco's proposal to Bruno created a dilemma: to either stay where he was – with security and a set salary – or risk setting up a branch from scratch. It sounded daunting. First off, it was not even possible to know how long that adventure could last. The branch would certainly not be bankrolled by Stefanini for a long while. Ultimately, it could just be a waste of time, and Bruno would end up coming back to São Paulo empty-handed.

Then, he had never worked as a salesman before (in that sense, he was similar to Márcio Da Mata, from the Bamerindus project). He had visited some clients in the last few months, but nothing that gave him much experience. A newcomer by all accounts, Bruno had the computer science course taken in Piracicaba in mind and a desire to work. At the time, a good technician had prospects in São Paulo. Now, a branch in the countryside without clients...

But what if he managed to attract some customers? Marco had promised to participate in the contracts, and eventually, he agreed. It seemed like it could work out. However, Bruno's journey to set up shop in the countryside wasn't as simple as taking his truck, table, chairs, and telephone and going there. There were significant obstacles to overcome before he could establish his office.

Bruno couldn't immediately set up a proper office because there were no clients to support the expenses. Initially, his office would be his car. To be able to travel around, he purchased an economical asset, a brand new bordeaux Volkswagen Gol that ran on alcohol. Bruno took on the role of a traveling salesman, conducting business from his car.

Accepting Marco's proposal and serving the São Paulo countryside required extensive travel. In the beginning, Bruno continued to visit important clients in the Greater São Paulo area, such as Unibanco, Itaú, and Telesp. He would hit the road between each visit.

The territory Bruno had to cover while on the road was vast. To the North, there was Ribeirão Preto; to the West, Sorocaba;

and to the East, São José dos Campos. However, his primary focus was on Campinas, which included numerous companies in significant municipalities like Piracicaba, Limeira, Americana, Itatiba, and Indaiatuba. Altogether, there were over 100 cities where potential Stefanini customers could be found.

And so, the exploration began. For months, Bruno relentlessly contacted the technology departments of various companies, almost begging for a meeting. When he finally succeeded, he introduced Stefanini and shared his experience with the only two clients he had served under the company's name: Magazine Luiza, which was under Mônica's responsibility, and Caterpillar, which was under Marco's responsibility.

The responses Bruno received from potential clients seemed repetitive, like a scratched record playing the same old hits. He encountered various common reactions. Ignorance was one of them, where people would say they had never heard of Stefanini and didn't know where the company was located. Another common response was the perfect world scenario, where companies claimed they were doing fine and didn't require any additional services. And then there was the poverty response, where companies would lament that they had already exhausted their budget for the year and couldn't allocate funds for anything else.

On top of these expected reactions, there was an unspoken implied answer that Bruno often sensed. The executives were hesitant to bring in outsiders, fearing that the company might disappear or close its branch. Some simply feared losing their jobs. Board members and managers were concerned that the department might shrink and lose importance in the company, becoming mere supervisors of third-party contracts. However, such fears were unfounded and rare, as managers are typically innovative and competent, unafraid of change.

While there were a few small local businesses providing occasional services, Bruno needed to secure a substantial and consistent contract for Stefanini. He aimed for a major and complex project that would span several months.

Bruno dedicated his entire day to the idea of establishing the branch, but he couldn't shake off the constant doubt of whether he was doing everything right. There were numerous potential pitfalls and concepts that needed to be transformed. Would the market be receptive to an unfamiliar company? Would companies be willing to hire a company they had never heard of? Would they embrace the concept of outsourcing important tasks?

"Maybe I'm completely mistaken about all this," Bruno pondered. "Perhaps I've set myself up for disappointment."

However, gradually Bruno began gathering information about the specific needs of companies, gaining an understanding of what it meant to do business in the countryside. He identified basic industries like Dedini in the Sertãozinho and Piracicaba regions. There were significant companies in the textile sector around Americana and other surrounding areas. Additionally, several automotive companies such as Varga, TRW, 3M, Case, Caterpillar, and Bosch operated in the region.

During that time, the executives at Bosch were grappling with the new reality of Mercosur, making adjustments to their production, processes, and systems in order to export products on time and meet the required standards. It was a period of immense transformation and revolution in the industry. While many employees saw it as a corporate crisis or a nuisance, Bruno saw it as a valuable opportunity. He believed that projects related to organizing the flow of foreign trade and ensuring quality control at the factory could be the entry points he was looking for.

During one of his visits, Bruno received a tip from an employee at Bosch. The company produced a wide range of vehicle-related items, including injection valves, control units, electrical components, and parts for diesel vehicles. At that time, Asian companies were just starting out and were nowhere near the quality achieved by the German industry. Winning over Bosch as a customer would be a significant achievement for Bruno and could justify opening the Stefanini branch in the São Paulo countryside.

The employee's tip specifically mentioned a man named Alexandre Winneschhofer, who was leading a project at Bosch. Alexandre, of Austrian descent, had joined Bosch in 1987 after graduating in systems analysis from PUC Campinas. He initially worked in systems development but later gained prominence and took on more responsibilities, including supervising the technological infrastructure of the company.

Alexandre's work was demanding, and he found himself dealing with people, a significant change from his previous focus on coding. He lived in Jardim Guanabara, close to Bosch, and followed a typical routine, arriving at the factory at 7 am and leaving at 5:45 pm. Even when he was at home, work didn't stop, and he was available 24/7 as part of the DPC (Data Processing Center).

The IT support at Bosch had already been outsourced to three small local suppliers, which provided quick responses and low costs. There were no strict audit controls at the time, unlike the current Sarbanes-Oxley Act (SOX) regulations. Alexandre valued the good prices and agility provided by these small suppliers, which aligned with Bosch's needs.

Given the characteristics of the IT support outsourcing, Bruno saw an opportunity for Stefanini to handle the data extraction project for Mercosur. He presented a proposal to Alexandre, and five days later, Bruno received a call from him, sealing the deal.

Ecstatic with the news, Bruno couldn't contain his excitement and joy. He screamed and shouted, even opening the car window to release his exhilaration. After months of traveling and facing countless rejections, Stefanini had finally secured a contract in the countryside. The company had achieved its goal of selling outside São Paulo.

After sharing the news with Marco, Bruno realized that the new client, Bosch, would serve as an excellent reference in the countryside market. This project went beyond just data extraction and justified the need for a physical branch for Stefanini. Bruno began the process by searching for an office location in Campinas that was easily accessible and had nearby amenities like restaurants, banks, and printing shops. After a few days of searching, he rented a 60 m2 office in downtown Campinas.

With the office space secured, the next step was to hire employees. Two professionals from Stefanini's headquarters in São Paulo, who had helped write the proposal, were sent to the new branch. They were initially accommodated in a nearby hotel for convenience. However, they soon discovered that the hotel was located in the red light district, with thin walls that allowed them to hear suggestive sounds from neighboring rooms. Bruno promptly went to rescue them from the situation.

Despite the initial hiccups, securing Bosch as a client made it easier for Bruno to show results to other companies in the region, given the industry's relevance. By the end of 1995, Bruno had won over eight clients. Within eight months, the branch was profitable, and Bruno could sustain it without depending on the headquarters in São Paulo. The client portfolio grew to include renowned companies such as Equipav, Fama, TRW (known as Varga at the time), and 3M. Bruno remained in the region until 2005, taking on responsibilities for the entire technical area at Stefanini and designing projects for other branches, often traveling to Rio de Janeiro, Curitiba, and Porto Alegre.

After leaving Stefanini, Bruno briefly worked a low-profile office job in São Paulo. However, in 2010, he returned to the roads and airports, traversing various parts of Brazil during the week. Despite not returning to Stefanini, Bruno's positive experience paved the way for Marco to hire other trailblazers and open new branches. Marco's sister, Mônica, began supervising offices in Campinas, Porto Alegre, and Curitiba in 1996, and more branches were established in Minas Gerais and Rio de Janeiro. Stefanini continued to expand, with Mônica becoming the queen of airports, traveling frequently to different branches.

However, each new branch faced similar challenges as Bruno's experience, lacking a strong local reference to offer companies in the region. Opening offices everywhere without sufficient financial backing was not feasible with a tight budget. For example, the Rio branch initially didn't even have furniture, and meetings had to be conducted while sitting on beach chairs.

Over time, the persistence of Mônica and managers like Bruno propelled Stefanini further than any other IT services company in Brazil. However, a new challenge awaited them, this time from within Stefanini itself, as they tackled the resistance associated with national expansion.

CHAPTER 9

FIEFDOM AND FACTORY

C rises are good, or so says the oft-repeated wisdom of corporate gurus. But forget speeches and PowerPoint slides. Forget the old Chinese proverb about opportunity. For a moment, let's set that whole theory aside. Let's get to the facts.

A lot happened in Brazil in that year of 1995. You could say that again. In 1994, the country was plagued by historic hyperinflation, and all Brazilians received news of another economic plan that would solve everything with skeptical ears. The Real Plan was the fifth and perhaps the weirdest and most complicated of all economic plans, including a "currency index", the URV, which required Brazilians to convert prices using a table. From that point onward, Brazil started to change. So did Stefanini.

The year 1995 witnessed Márcio Da Mata flying dozens of times towards Curitiba, in addition to Bruno Mondin traveling the roads of the São Paulo countryside hundreds of times. It was the time of explorers. In São Paulo, that same year, a different form of learning began for Stefanini employees. But in this case, it had nothing to do with expansion; it was a matter of centralizing, of concentrating everything in one place. A matter of hiring!

Aparecida Bondezan ran a bar in Belo Horizonte before starting to work for Stefanini. She arrived that summer of 1995 and was soon visiting clients. At the time, she knew nothing about computers, but one could definitely say she handled people well. One of the first customers was the Lloyds bank, on the corner of Avenida Brigadeiro Faria Lima and Avenida Rebouças (where the Brasilinvest building is located today). The pivotal moment for her would be in early March 1995, shortly after Carnival. Marco's sister, Mônica, worked with Lloyds, and it was she who took Aparecida to see the bank that had changed the history of information technology in Brazil. The two parked their car, entered the elevator, and Mônica pressed the button for the 18th and last floor, the penthouse. There, they would meet the executive responsible for all the bank's technology: Cláudio Bacchi.

Mônica, Aparecida, and Cláudio met to finalize the details of an extremely important contract for Stefanini. However, before explaining the content of this contract, it is worth going back in time and understanding why Lloyds was so crucial for the entire Brazilian market, especially in the information technology segment. As well as the dimension of the challenge that Stefanini would face.

Few banks have managed to match the prestige of Lloyds in Brazil. Its first operations here date back to 1918 when the bank bought financial houses so old that many of them had begun to operate under the signature of Emperor Dom Pedro II. When it arrived in Brazil, Lloyds had existed for 150 years in England. Perhaps because of all its pomp and tradition, it built a proud structure in a continental country.

Proud, in this case, is an adjective that can characterize both a virtue and a defect. In the 1980s, there were 16 branches of this English bank in Brazil. Or – as more daring types would say – 16 Lloyds in operation, each with their own infrastructure, accounting, leaders, language, and ways of running the business.

This configuration was the byproduct of a time when communication was difficult, and waiting for orders and counterorders meant missing opportunities. Furthermore, the proximity of the branches in the North and Northeast to the Northern Hemisphere made them more "intimate" with developed countries and less accustomed to subjecting themselves to the orders of executives in the Southeast. Thus, if Nitro Química could be considered the pinnacle of the do-it-all-yourself model, Lloyds was a monument to decentralization. With all the good and bad that come with this option of giving power, resources, and autonomy to the extremities, of course.

The physical and material aspect of each branch aptly expressed that reality. Almost all branches acquired buildings considered by the employees themselves to be "sumptuous." The Rio de Janeiro branch had 2,500 employees (it would later operate with 13).

That was the reality in the mid-1980s. And, in the same year when Marco graduated, in the midst of the economic crisis, in 1987, engineer Cláudio Bacchi left the Arthur Andersen consultancy and arrived at the English bank.

The previous year, Lloyds had hired Arthur Andersen to carry out a restructuring of the bank. In the Brazilian market, no one spoke of downsizing yet, and the concept of process reengineering would only be disseminated a decade later. But Lloyds needed to recycle itself. Downsizing alone wouldn't cut it; a different type of cut would be required.

The first movement was the simplest and most physical: getting rid of the apparent wealth – real estate. Cláudio Bacchi himself was in charge of selling several buildings. Even the headquarters moved from Rua XV de Novembro to Avenida Brigadeiro Faria Lima, at the South Tower, where it occupied the penthouse on the 18th floor and six more floors. There, a new type of center was created. Lloyds converged to that point. It was the start of the contraction process.

Reducing the physical aspect was relatively simple; after all, a few fewer buildings haven't changed Lloyds' service. Systems development, in turn, has always been seen as the heart of the financial business. Banks would hire battalions of employees who spent hours discussing and crunching lines of code. Each manager's appreciation for their information workers made them resemble artisans; each area had its own group of analysts and developers. And these groups operated as small fiefdoms. Convincing corporations and executives to relinquish this contingent became a Machiavellian battle, even more painful than extirpating internal computing support or downsizing the mainframe to desktops.

But Stefanini did not face a conflicted Lloyds in 1995. In reality, the English bank quickly took a cue from the market since, at the end of the 1980s, the situation had begun to change. Cláudio, inspired and indoctrinated by his consulting time at Arthur Andersen, warned area coordinators that the individual software development teams would end. The end of fiefdoms was near. The basic idea was to concentrate development in a programming pool, something that would later be known as a software factory.

Most rejected this new idea, claiming it would compromise their agility. High inflation demanded swift changes to the system, and this had to be done by analysts with specific training and knowledge to work in the department and better develop the application logic. "A programmer in the hand is worth five in the pool" was the refrain the executives repeated, claiming that this was the formula for being competitive in Brazil at that time. The opposite logic was to bring everyone together under one group to get better results from the available professionals.

After much discussion, the area coordinators agreed on the programmer pool. From that point on, they were forced to plan for the future. If they didn't plan out, they no longer had programmers at their behest at any time. The scenario changed, different processes were differently prioritized, and an internal committee was created with decision-making power and clear governance criteria.

In 1995, the Lloyds development pool faced issues with the quality of the outsourced company, putting Lloyds' pioneering spirit at risk. Mônica Stefanini, who provided language and mainframe training services for Lloyds, saw an opportunity to prove herself and earn a contract for Stefanini. It was a gamble made by Cláudio Bacchi, as Stefanini had never taken on software development for a company, especially not for an important bank like Lloyds, which had created a pool and a governability model for efficient software production in Brazil.

Taking on the responsibility of IT support for a company and migrating the entire mainframe infrastructure to smaller platforms was a major challenge for Marco Stefanini's team. Additionally, expanding the services of a São Paulo company to other states was also daunting. However, the Lloyds contract meant much more—it involved manufacturing the essential codes for a major bank and playing a central role in organizing and managing the flow of clients' money. Stefanini would be at the heart of Lloyds' operations.

To manage the development, Mônica reached out to Adalberto Tolino, who had extensive experience with mainframes, the Cobol language, and large databases. Adalberto initially declined the invitation, as he enjoyed the stability and appreciated his work at Fepasa. However, when Fepasa faced privatization, with the company being sold at an auction,

Adalberto reconsidered and called Mônica to accept the offer from Stefanini.

Meanwhile, Aparecida had closed her bar in Belo Horizonte and joined Stefanini in São Paulo. She and Mônica faced difficulties and desperation in finding a professional with enough experience and knowledge to run Lloyds' software factory. They realized that finding someone with that profile would be challenging since companies wouldn't willingly let go of such skilled professionals.

In mid-April 1995, Fepasa experienced a significant shakeup due to privatization. Over 10,000 employees left the company, mostly through layoffs. Adalberto saw the situation at Fepasa deteriorate and decided to call Mônica to inquire about the offer for Lloyds. Luckily, the offer still stood, and he accepted it, marking a turning point in his career.

Adalberto would move from a state-owned company with centuries-old assets to a private and family-owned company opened eight years prior in Brazil and with 250 employees. This was big news for Stefanini as well: Mônica had just hired the first manager of the software factory.

Since Lloyds was located on the corner of Faria Lima and Rebouças, Adalberto decided to move from downtown São Paulo to the Jardins neighborhood. He could arrive faster at the bank from there. Adalberto's concern with speed was a good call. He would soon see that things moved at a very different pace at Lloyds.

On his first day, Adalberto pressed the elevator button for the tenth floor, made sure there was already a table and chair there, and sat down. For a brief moment. Adalberto spent weeks walking from floor to floor, department to department, listening in endless meetings to what clients from different areas had to

97

say and trying to understand the world of Lloyds' systems. And there was a lot to wrap his head around.

First barrier: IT had already been downsized there, unlike what happened at Fepasa. Cláudio Bacchi started the downsizing process in 1991 and ended it just before Aparecida and Adalberto arrived in 1994. Since then, there had been no mainframe at Lloyds. Everything was now running in those small closed black boxes, something that did not exist at Fepasa.

Second barrier: Lloyds' management was very different from that of a state-owned company. With fewer employees and the rush of the private sector, everything was done quickly and without that many protocols. At Fepasa, there was a lot of bureaucracy, but, in exchange, there were gains in terms of organization (incidentally, something that meshed well with the mainframe, an environment that is averse to mess). Adalberto realized that he had grown up with information technology in a clean and organized world.

Finally, the highest barrier of all: the jungle of software and systems, standards and platforms, manufactured over the years by the information artisans and their fiefdoms and further nurtured and extended by the pool. Yes, even imploding the physical fiefdoms into the pool hadn't completely solved the problem. The myriad code written in eleven different languages prevented the pool itself from operating efficiently. And everything depended on the pool: customer registration, accounting, balance sheets, collection, loans, active funds, practically all the tasks of a bank the size of Lloyds. It was as if the different languages reproduced the 16 "sumptuous" branches in the virtual realm. This virtual chaos would provide Adalberto with the greatest challenge of his career.

To cross the forest, Adalberto had almost no map, or that which programmers call documentation. It is worth explaining to lay readers: when a good programmer writes a line of code, anyone else who sits in their chair will immediately understand what they did. The logic is simple, the variable is never X or Z, but rather a self-explanatory name like "account1" or "defaultzero"; most importantly, there's always a comment at strategic points in the code detailing how it works and what the goal of that section is. The Lloyds jungle lacked any of that; it was something akin to being hurled right into the middle of the Amazon without a compass or a map.

Adalberto didn't know the forest for the trees, so to speak; he was not familiar with almost any of the languages used at Lloyds. But that wasn't why Mônica hired the Araraquara native. Adalberto knew how to organize; he knew how to create logic from chaos.

Two weeks after arriving, the manager realized that the chaos went further than he could comprehend.

– I give up! Can anyone help me understand what is wrong? – said Adalberto, a few semitones higher than usual, to the programmer sitting at a table opposite his. He walked around and sat beside her, staring at the screen full of colors and flashing options, an incomprehensible sight for him, used to the dry world of Cobol codes.

Without understanding almost any of that, Adalberto said in a tone that only the programmer heard: – Go on... explain to me what the problem is.

Fifteen minutes later, when he finally understood – and accepted it –, he couldn't believe it. The software did make changes to the database, but it didn't leave any traces indicating whether the information had been saved, altered, or whatnot. To Adalberto's organized mind, that sounded like an offense recorded on magnetic signals. Everything would be more complicated than it seemed at first.

It wasn't all bad; there was something extremely positive in it for Adalberto and for Stefanini. The governability of the pool created within Lloyds offered a functional process, and the criteria for what should be done gave the team direction. In this quarter, the priority was the balance sheet; in the next, the investment funds. The internal committee set the direction, and the Stefanini team moved forward.

After two years of exhausting toil, the systems were finally unified, the problems were solved, and Stefanini – with Adalberto leading the team – started to establish standards to be followed, no matter what language was used. The last barrier fell, the virtual fiefdom was finally dismantled, and the English bank began to operate as an efficient factory. At the same time, without picking up a reference book on the syntax of languages, but always monitoring programmers' questions and identifying logic errors, Adalberto gradually learned the basics of the languages used at Lloyds. Most importantly, Stefanini gained experience and fame by leading a development pool with numerous complex projects for the main market of information technology: the financial system.

The team was recognized to the point where they were all treated like Lloyds employees; they received gifts like the in-house workers, they were invited to parties, sometimes everyone forgot that Adalberto's team was outsourced. The former fiefdoms now looked very favorably on the pool staff, and the "Stefaninis" were at home at Lloyds. But not quite.

The year 1996 was half over, and one morning, one of the programmers told Adalberto that he wanted to leave because Lojas Marisa had made him an offer. Two hours later, a queue formed... everyone wanted to quit. Eleven employees at once – there would be virtually no one left in the pool.

Adalberto picked up the phone, dialed and spoke in a low voice:

– Aparecida, call Mônica and tell her to come here quickly; my team has decided to jump ship.

The two women were at the Stefanini office in the Cal Center building, also on Avenida Faria Lima, and arrived at Lloyds in 19 minutes. Talking to the team, they discovered that there was no dissatisfaction, just tempting offers, all of which came from the same place. And it wasn't exactly from Lojas Marisa, but from a competitor that was entering a contract with the retail chain in the São Paulo countryside.

After convincing the team of the advantages of staying, not without renegotiating pay with some of them, Mônica scheduled a meeting at the Lojas Marisa office in the Barra Funda neighborhood. Two days later, the contract with Lojas Marisa went to Stefanini.

Other banks, such as Bradesco, contributed greatly to the software factory model. However, the experience of Stefanini and Lloyds, in addition to being relevant in the Brazilian market, allowed Marco to acquire knowledge that no other IT services company would obtain for a long time. Something that would later become the face and future of Stefanini in Brazil. But before that, the efficiency of the assembly line would need to be reviewed. A new crisis was causing a revolution; this time, it had nothing to do with the economy but with the pressure of the competition.

CHAPTER 10

ULTIMATUM

I am a programmer, I don't have to chase other people's signatures.

The sentence was addressed to the person responsible for organizing the processes, Carlos Correa Henrique, who heard the voice but did not see the employee's eyes, as the outburst was uttered while the programmer walked away and left the room. Carlos lowered his head and tried to slow down his heartbeat. That had been a tense year at Stefanini. Work and relationships changed and would never be the same as before.

The programmer's outburst occurred in the first half of 1996, at the height of the company's transformation, attempting to formalize processes and with its owner being forced to put business before friendship. Stefanini was changing profoundly.

Not all entrepreneurs manage to make this shift, and very few do it willingly. In general, this only happens as a matter of survival. So it was with Marco, by force.

And not all that sudden. The danger and change came slowly, and with them came the reaction. Ten years after Marco entered the IT field, he still seemed less like the owner of a promising national company and more like a friend you would meet for a beer, hesitant to confront old and competent employees. He faced crises, changed the culture of the market, and expanded the company nationwide. But he was slow to react when it was necessary to fire someone, when he needed to push employees, he knew to be competent to their limit, but who nevertheless had to bend to standards and meet deadlines. It's not that Marco was lenient; he wouldn't have gotten there without being a good manager, without knowing how to lead and choose good managers and professionals. But he and all the managers would make occasional exceptions – he'd cut slack for competent employees, and they'd do so for clients, who would ask from Stefanini and it would comply, without caring much about processes. It was time to break the bond of personal relationships.

The timing was not by Marco's choice. The need for change came from an external pressure on Stefanini. After the technology market opened, Brazil was invaded by IT multinationals. Competition intensified; companies such as IBM and EDS invested to win over customers they had in other countries in Brazil, while corporations from other sectors brought their own service providers, such as Philips, which brought its fellow Dutch company BSO/Origin. National groups reacted and invested in their own companies: Bradesco with CPM and Scopus; Itaú with Itautec; the Bunge Brasil Group with Proceda (currently part of the Tivit group).

Among these giants, Stefanini was still a small company, medium-sized at best. When it came to closing deals, firepower made the difference. Competitors such as IBM used sophisticated tools to design projects; Stefanini continued to use in-house processes because it didn't have the money to afford these tools and couldn't pass the costs on to its clients. Multinationals were able to spread software costs across global customers; Stefanini was obliged to charge less and less for its services in order to win over the Brazilian market.

In everyday life, difficulties began to make life more difficult for Marco and all employees. With better tools, better processes, and a larger client base, major competitors knew exactly how much a project would cost, how long it would take, in addition to all the costs involved. At Stefanini, the lack of a single, organized methodology made every project a risk – a reluctant shot hoping for a target.

Strangled by the market, Marco earned less on contracts and demanded increasingly more from his employees. One of those who felt the increased pressure was Marco's former colleague from Bradesco, Luiz Edmundo, who decided to leave the company in 1994 and return to Informatel.

Marco realized he had to do something.

In the last few recent years, Marco's father had suffered his own business crisis. Milton ran a downsized Lampo Products after being beaten down by tougher competition and a tougher market. In the high inflation environment, four years earlier, Produtos Lampo was forced to move from Guarulhos to Barueri, where it started paying rent again. From 40 employees, the number dropped to less than half of that.

The problem originated from a strategic error. In the good times, Milton felt virtually no competitive pressure. Even after discovering that some companies offered the same products to its customers, Lampo stayed its course. The lack of innovation made the company vulnerable.

With the economy in bad shape, Milton had to cut costs. From direct sales to stores, he moved on to distributors. But the competition was also meeting with these distributors, and the products were the same. The vulnerability increased. With that, major buyers of distributors, such as Mesbla and Mappin, went bankrupt; the damage moved along the production chain until it reached Milton. They started asking for 120 days to pay, sometimes up to six months. Fragilized and lacking funds, he became a sitting duck. Milton considered shutting Lampo Products down.

Marco closely followed the problem experienced by his father, seeing how difficult it was to face the crisis without being prepared, without having an advantage and a special relationship with the market. Stefanini couldn't afford to be so vulnerable.

They offered good price and quality, but the market asked for something more tangible, a guarantee of delivery before delivery. When a service is sold, the buyer does not see the product. They need to believe that everything will turn out well and close the deal in the dark. Innovating at that time meant providing security.

Marco would have to find ways around the lack of money and still organize the company more professionally. For the task, he would need the support of people focused on the method, on organization, and in quality processes. It wasn't about finding better professionals – Stefanini had those; it was about having a different mentality.

The person with these characteristics had arrived at Stefanini at the end of 1994. Carlos Henrique had always been a technology enthusiast. He entered the Technological Institute of Aeronautics (ITA) in 1980 at the age of 20. He took a two-year technologist course with extensive emphasis on software, one of the few places where students directly operated large mainframes (this was four years before Marco ever approached a large computer at Bradesco). At ITA, Carlos learned the concept of processes very well because the course provided a good introduction to the subject. He pursued a career in technology and, for four years, worked at the computer manufacturing companies Brascom and Digirede.

It was at his next job, at Promon, that Carlos formed his personality, profile, and career. As an engineering company, the managerial spirit there translated into very organized processes.

That is why, before doing anything at Promon, Carlos spent two months reading the company's rules. Then, four more months studying the extensive tome that contained Arthur Andersen's Foundation methodology, a classic at the time. In 1992, Carlos spent Christmas with a head full of processes.

However, in early 1994, Carlos already felt underutilized at Promon. A colleague who was a consultant at Stefanini recommended him to integrate the Santa Marina databases of the Saint Gobain Group. Carlos accepted the job and, for six months, made the journey from his home in Santo André to Freguesia do Ó, where the glass company was located, to evaluate the best databases available at the time (those in the know will recognize names brands such as Oracle, Sybase, and Informix). He made such a thorough report that it impressed the client. In the end, Marco invited Carlos to chat and to get to know him more closely.

Marco's motivation at the time still had nothing to do with the problem of Stefanini's methods, but with the need to have professionals with attested mastery of technologies to impress clients when selling projects. He was looking for someone who also knew SQL, Microsoft's database, and who could prove their knowledge. Carlos had never touched the software before, but he considered himself an expert on Sybase, which had been the inspiration for SQL.

– I've never worked with it – he confessed at the time. – But I can pass the certification anyhow.

At Stefanini, some thought that Carlos was too boastful, and others even made informal bets stating that he would not pass. Carlos did pass. A week later, with his SQL certificate in hand, in July 1994, Carlos entered the Cal Center building to transform the company.

In just under two months, life began to change at Stefanini. Marco's guideline was that processes needed to become more precise right from the start, and Carlos began to put his theory into practice. Until then, projects allowed for errors of up to 40% in cost forecasting. Should they err on the positive side, they ran the risk of losing the contract because it was too expensive; if they undershot the mark, they would lose money.

Carlos' slogan was: the more details foreseen in the project, the smaller the margin of error. It sounds obvious but is quite complicated to execute. Without being intimidated, the ITA alumnus went on to define, in detail, what the team would be like, the type of professionals, the required experience, the level of knowledge; in the project, he defined software platforms and additional tools needed. It was work – a lot of work – just to design something that was a mere proposal, a promise with no guarantees. But it was worthwhile: the margin of error dropped to 20%. More wins, fewer losses.

In his third month at work, Carlos had the chance to put the method to the test. Pharmaceutical company Novartis – at the time called Ciba – tendered for a service. Stefanini's competitor said it could deliver in three months, and Carlos cautioned the client, convinced that seven months would be more accurate. Stefanini won the contract, delivered, gained customer satisfaction, and internally, Carlos was held in higher esteem.

The following year, in 1995, Luiz Edmundo returned to Stefanini and found a changed company, with processes actually being adhered to, higher earnings, and a smaller number of conflicts with employees.

But the worst and hardest was yet to come. Alright, a lot had improved as far as the schedule and the project were concerned, but the execution had slipped. When one phase evolves, the next one becomes problematic. One bottleneck is eliminated, others appear. In this case, it became clear that it was also possible to greatly improve the quality of the results. It also became clear that one of the bottlenecks was located in staff selection. After winning the contract and in a rush to serve the client, the manager in charge ended up hiring a technician or programmer without the necessary experience, without mastery over crucial tools for the project to be executed. A better, more documented process would prevent simple mistakes like these. There was a lack of method.

However, if so much work was required to change the way of putting project proposals together, imagine improving quality in the nick of time, during delivery, in real-life circumstances. It would be an inconceivable amount of additional work, and more work meant a higher price when billing customers. Carlos Henrique studied Arthur Andersen's models and knew how to do it, but he soon realized that, in order to achieve the same rigor as the North American consulting firm, he would need to greatly increase Stefanini's costs. A five-person job would require ten people. By then, clients could prefer to hire a multinational company to the detriment of the medium-sized national company.

There was a different way forward, however. Since the beginning of the 1990s, a new fever was spreading through Brazilian companies. The market was quickly becoming more professional, largely due to globalization, which brought fierce competition between companies from all countries and increased quality standards. This trend translated into a quality certification called ISO 9000.

In 1989, the German company Siemens was the first to implement this certification in Brazil. It makes perfect sense that a German company would be the first to obtain a quality certification. The first German organization focused on defining standards dates back to 1869. It is not myth or exaggeration; organization is truly at the heart of German culture.

Strictly speaking, the quality standards we know today were also the result of a reaction to that same German culture. During the first and second world wars, British soldiers realized that German weapons were better. This was a major issue because if a machine gun jammed, a grenade didn't explode, or a tank broke down, battles and lives would be lost. At that time, quality standards received great encouragement from the British government, and a few decades later, these same standards would give rise to ISO 9000. German competitors made the British (and later the whole world) evolve and invest in quality. The crisis took the form of an extremely competent aggressor who imposed an ultimatum: improve or die.

ISO 9001, the first globally adopted corporate standard, was issued in 1987. In Germany, Siemens distributed the document internally for its employees to read. Currently, when executives decide to adopt a new process, they establish a one- or two-year goal. At Siemens, however, everything was already set (it was easy, after all, Siemens itself had been one of the main models for preparing the ISO 9001).

Two years later, the Brazilian subsidiary followed the same path. There was no accredited certifying body, and the National Institute of Metrology, Quality, and Technology (Inmetro) took on that role. Inspectors spent a week at the Lapa factory, the first to be certified. The inaugural Brazilian ISO 9001 was issued on December 4, 1989. Within a few years, corporate fever had spread, and by 1995, every company was planning to get certified. Over time, all sorts of businesses would seek certification. However, in the beginning, the main interested parties were companies that sold products to other businesses. Marketing's biggest gain lay in the ability to proudly show customers a certificate that few possessed, providing that extra push when signing a contract. Marketing was the driver.

Stefanini's customers themselves were infected by the fever and sought certifications attesting to quality. Even public sector customers began to favor certified suppliers.

With the ISO 9000 hullabaloo, Marco decided to follow the same path. If the IT sector's options were too expensive and being empty-handed was not an option, the way forward was to bend the rules of the game. Many people in the market found it strange and even quaint that no software company was certified in any variation of ISO 9000. When it was time to choose, Stefanini's team discovered that there was a specific ISO for services, 9002, but the one for industries was even more comprehensive. Marco chose to apply for ISO 9001, the toughest one.

Industries took from one to two years in the certification process, and each one approached it differently. Marco hired a consultancy and, internally, selected a professional to lead the project: Carlos Henrique.

Refining the process to eliminate the possibility of error required someone detail-oriented and meticulous like an engineer. Carlos was the right person to organize that, but it was necessary to find someone like him at the other end, a professional that Carlos could observe in the field and create a model to be followed. He needed a guinea pig.

The most diligent person at the time was Argentinean Federico Mauro, who had come to Brazil and married a Brazilian woman. In 1993, they decided to settle down in Brazil, and Federico knocked on several doors for months in search of a job. Stefanini was the seventh door he knocked on.

By the time Carlos joined the company in 1994, Federico was already one of Stefanini's commercial managers. Like Carlos,

Federico was organized and logical, although he had a slightly different profile as he was also involved in painting, playing the guitar, and singing.

For several months, Carlos accompanied Federico in meetings, often on weekends, trying to understand every detail of the paperwork for projects at different stages. The clear, correct, and perfect path to be followed was crystallized into a succinct 35-page document.

In those pages, Carlos described in the simplest possible way how things should be run at Stefanini. The document aimed for brevity, avoiding wordiness or excess. Employees were expected to use those 35 pages as a quick guide. However, when applied to a live project, those same 35 single-sided sheets transformed into a massive tome of hundreds and hundreds of pages. Filling out so many pages became a problem and a significant annoyance for each Stefanini employee. This effort, which aimed to ensure quality assurance, also became the biggest internal conflict that Marco's young company would face.

The new processes controlled every step taken by Stefanini's managers, programmers, and salespeople. No one could hire, fire, start, or finish a project without faithfully observing Carlos Henrique's new 35-page gospel. The gospel required everything to be registered and signed by all parties involved, from the programmer to the client. However, the new gospel was still just a stack of paper.

Ignoring the document did not mean harboring ill will towards Stefanini or desiring to sabotage Marco's company. It simply indicated that each individual had their own approach to project management, and in the midst of daily challenges, decisions that may inadvertently harm others can seem justified. For instance, cell managers would often overlook employees assigned to smaller contracts for weeks. If an issue arose and an employee resigned, it became difficult to find a replacement since the manager had no knowledge of the ongoing work. However, Federico, an attentive team member, consistently visited the three main clients on a weekly or fortnightly basis. He actively engaged with clients, listened to their concerns about man-hours and employees' requests for pay raises. Federico diligently monitored all aspects of the projects, while Carlos meticulously recorded everything in the quality gospel.

In general, mistakes arose from the desire to improve efficiency and profitability for Stefanini. Employees would prioritize agility, focusing on important clients or professionals who came highly recommended. However, this approach sometimes compromised precision, particularly with smaller clients or professionals who lacked the required experience for specific projects.

Hiring proved to be a weak point in the service execution. Selecting the wrong person resulted in steeper learning curves than anticipated for the projects. Issues would arise, costs would escalate, and time would be wasted.

Armed with the 35-page document, Carlos Henrique traversed the cells, conversing with managers and randomly inspecting documents to ensure compliance with standards. During this process, he encountered a sheet lacking the client's signature and sought out the responsible programmer. The programmer responded:

– Obtaining signatures from others is not part of my role; it is not my responsibility.

Employees still hadn't fully grasped the significance of their contributions toward maintaining a smoothly running company. Carlos Henrique sensed that things were going awry, with failure looming close by.

With just over 30 days remaining for the assessment that would determine whether Stefanini would be granted or denied ISO 9001 certification, two consultants from the contracted company arrived at the office for the final evaluation. This visit represented a last-ditch effort before the decisive moment. Over the course of two days, the consultants scrutinized contracts, reviewed meeting minutes, compared schedules, and examined resumes. Each requested document made Carlos Henrique apprehensive; he never expected the consultants to be so meticulous. With each document, more flaws surfaced, irrefutable evidence that Stefanini's culture remained unchanged and employees were resistant to altering their established ways. Ultimately, Carlos Henrique became convinced of an impending failure, leaving no choice but to cancel the certification.

Such an outcome would be disastrous, especially considering that the market was aware of the certification process and held expectations. Partners, customers, and competitors alike were cognizant of it. Achieving certification would undoubtedly be a triumph, a powerful asset in the marketing arena. However, failure would provide competitors with an opportunity to assail Stefanini, highlighting purported insurmountable quality and delivery issues, even if those claims were unfounded (which they were). The tables would turn against Marco.

In times like these, the underlying mechanisms of evolution become more apparent. Charles Darwin comprehended this concept upon discovering tortoises living in isolation on the Galapagos Islands. These creatures remained unchanged because they faced no threat from predators. Stefanini was not an island, despite some employees occasionally behaving as though it were. It was time to apply natural selection within the office environment.

Informed of the consultancy's verdict, Marco summoned his top managers. Twenty individuals attended the meeting, all fixating their gaze on a determined businessman. There was no water, coffee, or even cookies. Marco had something to say, and this time he had no need to entertain suggestions. He was well-acquainted with the problem and already had a solution in mind.

Standing at the head of the table, locking eyes with each participant, Marco commenced speaking with a tone that vividly conveyed his irritation and exasperation. He emphasized the importance of the certification, how it was vital for securing more contracts and how failing to obtain it would result in losing out to both expensive multinational corporations and cheap, low-quality domestic businesses. Stefanini needed to demonstrate that it was the superior choice compared to either of them.

– The consultants have proposed postponing the assessment until the end of the year. I rejected that notion. I will allow a maximum postponement of 30 days.

On the left side of the table, Carlos Henrique was taken aback by Marco's announcement. It seemed highly improbable that everything could be rectified in such a short period of less than two months. However, Marco had more to convey:

– Now, listen carefully and make it known to everyone: anyone who fails to adhere to the correct procedures within 15 days prior to the evaluation will be dismissed from Stefanini.

This time, the pledge was upheld. The individual who was affable with everyone, demanding yet supportive of colleagues, had a business to run, and this was the sole means of survival. The crisis in the competitive landscape had placed Stefanini at a crucial juncture, and only the best would continue to thrive.

The ultimatum had a transformative effect. Programmers diligently obtained signatures, managers made hiring decisions based on qualifications rather than solely relying on recommendations, and the entire work culture and approach underwent a complete overhaul. In July 1996, the assessment took place, and Stefanini was officially declared as the first technology services company in Brazil to achieve ISO 9001 certification. The processes were now officially validated, providing ammunition in the battle against competition, particularly against multinational corporations. Marco realized that this was just the beginning. It was time to shift from a defensive stance to an offensive one.

CHAPTER 11

GLOBAL

Antonio Moreira checked his watch for the twentieth time. An hour late, waiting at the front desk, all just to grab that Kimberly-Clark executive's attention. Rio Grande do Sul native Antonio had flown early from Florida to that meeting in Atlanta, Georgia, after three weeks of badgering, until he managed to speak with the executive and arrange that meeting. One hour later, the secretary came towards him a second time. Perhaps it was now time; but what he heard was:

"I'm sorry, sir, but he had a scheduling issue..."

Antonio had been employed at Stefanini since the beginning of 2001. All that effort to get a single meeting with an IT executive was not something that was part of the routine of Stefanini executives in Brazil. After all, the company had grown a lot over the past seven years. National expansion now reached branches in nine states, with 1,200 consultants and a huge variety of services and projects. Stefanini had grown so much that it faced the multinationals head on, taking contracts from all of them. Overseas, however, the name Stefanini meant nothing. And a nothing – or a nobody – tends to have a hard time arranging meetings with important executives.

And why would a company and its executives subject themselves to starting from scratch, as if all its recent achievements meant nothing? The answer is quite obvious for any business student: globalization is irreversible. It would be a huge waste of time for us to restate the arguments and reasons for a company to go international. Even the most lay reader knows why a company can no longer afford to stay within its borders; either it grows and swallows the others or it is swallowed up. International trade had been an entrepreneurial choice from the medieval times of the Italian Marco Polo until as recently as the 1980s. Then, communism ended, the Iron Curtain fell, and the world got too big for companies to sit around waiting for the competition to come knocking. Time to load your weapons, no one can escape the fray.

With the quality certification, Marco won his first important defense and showed the market that a national IT company could offer assurance. He was a trailblazer in this regard. But that alone wouldn't cut it. Multinationals still had an unmatched scale and deep pockets.

Interestingly, the idea of taking the Stefanini name to other markets was already quite old. During the Collor Plan, in 1990, when Marco was trying to get back on his feet, he and Graça even went to Argentina to clear their heads and investigate a budding offer of providing training programs at the IBM offices there. He visited the local branch of the North American partner, thinking of using a model similar to the one in Brazil. That didn't work. Five years later, still carrying the idea of operating in the foreign market, Marco opened a branch with two Argentineans, but the venture also ended up leading to more issues than benefits. Maybe it was the wrong moment, maybe the problem was Argentina – ultimately, doing business outside Brazil seemed too complicated.

Five more years passed before Marco decided to start an international adventure once again. In 2000, he asked all his managers to talk to clients and ask for referrals to contacts abroad. Two types were of interest: 1) Brazilian companies with branches large enough to require individual IT projects; and 2) multinational clients in Brazil who could refer Stefanini's services to the headquarters or other branches. It seemed like a good idea, something doable. It wasn't. Few managers got any referrals.

One of the few who did – two referrals, at least – was the Rio Grande do Sul native Antonio Moreira, the man left for dead at the waiting room at the start of this chapter. The executive was the business manager of the branch in Porto Alegre and had worked for Stefanini since 1997. Before that, he was a systems analyst and boosted his career by becoming director of RioSoft, a company born out of the IT department of the pulp manufacturer RioCell (acquired by Klabin and later by Aracruz). The experience at RioSoft was worthwhile. After all, Antonio had experience both on the client side – while the department was still part of the pulp manufacturer – and on the other side of the counter – when the company became independent. Understanding the interests and needs of both parties gave the analyst true business insight.

That was the part that helped Antonio stand out in Brazil. However, global executives are made from a different fabric, they have a different experience. The thing that opened Antonio's eyes to the global market was a project in Sweden, where he stayed for two months in 1991.

From there, he attended a postgraduate course in France, where he studied systems development methodology at the famous Telecom Bretagne (perhaps you may not know it, but this college is one of the most important schools in the European market when it comes to technology). Anyway, in 1997, the RioSoft team started working at Stefanini, and Antonio became the director of the Rio Grande do Sul branch.

Nothing out of the ordinary so far; Antonio really did have two interesting characteristics: business acumen and international experience. There was, however, a less obvious element: the fact that he proved to be an executive with initiative in Porto Alegre, far from Stefanini's headquarters in São Paulo. Why, a little to the South in Brazil or a lot to the North (in the United States) didn't make such a difference. What mattered was that the executive needed to know how to make fast decisions, how to deal with the forced autonomy of not having someone by his side pressing for results. That's why Mônica thought of Antonio when there was a need to choose someone to break into the United States market.

And that's how it all began. In September 2000, Antonio headed to the United States for the first time and stayed for a week. In October, he came back for the same period. In December, he went and stayed for good.

Antonio's work in 2001 would be very similar to what Bruno Mondin did in the São Paulo countryside in 1995. But, while the road was Bruno's office, Antonio's home would be the plane, reminiscent of Monica's years jumping from airport to airport in the branches throughout Brazil. From his office set up in Fort Lauderdale, Florida, the Porto Alegre native would have to cover the entire United States market.

Before boarding a plane, the first barrier to overcome would be to break through the fence that is set up against every Brazilian company: arranging a simple meeting. Therein lies the issue: what American or European would ever associate the country of samba, soy, beer, beaches, soccer, and bikini-clad women with methodical technology services? The idea still stumps many today. Ten years ago, it seemed insane.

Yes, many Brazilian companies had already entered small IT contracts around the world. Nothing all that relevant. At the time, no Brazilian trade mission by a technology company had attempted to explore developed markets in an organized fashion. It was only two years later that the first organized attempt took place, albeit in a merely exploratory capacity. Twenty Brazilian companies, including Stefanini, went to the State of Virginia, in September 2002, to try and get a better grasp of the United States market. They came home empty-handed but with learning in their heads.

So, in the beginning of 2001, Marco and Antonio were pioneers in their field. However, they faced challenges due to the weak reputation of the Brazil brand in the industry and the lack of reference clients. They were caught in the classic dilemma of not being able to acquire clients because they didn't have any yet, and not having any clients because of this reason. They needed to find a solution to this problem.

To start off, Antonio and a secretary established the branch with limited resources. They had a list of around 50 executives from US companies and began making calls to potential clients. One of their targets was Omar Postigo, who was in charge of Odebrecht's IT department in Miami, United States. After a few days of negotiation, they successfully secured a contract with Omar, who was dissatisfied with their previous supplier. This was a significant achievement for Stefanini.

However, this initial success was not enough to establish Stefanini's reputation in the US market. The contract they obtained was small, short-term, and for a Brazilian company. They needed more substantial accomplishments to make a name for themselves in the United States.

The following months were challenging, with numerous attempts that didn't yield significant results. The situation became even more difficult after the terrorist attack on September 11, 2001, which led to an economic crisis. Executives had less time to consider unknown Brazilian companies and preferred to stick with their trusted suppliers, who offered good deals and discounts. The fear of trying something different made Antonio question the feasibility of exploring the US market.

While Antonio faced rejection in the United States, an unprecedented event was occurring in Brazil. In 2001, Jairo Avritchir, an executive at Dell in Brazil, proposed the idea of establishing a software factory in Rio Grande do Sul to the company's North American headquarters. Jairo highlighted the advantages of Brazil's Information Technology Law, which reduced professional costs to levels comparable to India. He also emphasized the country's devalued currency, making everything even more cost-effective.

Jairo presented studies demonstrating that Brazil had cheap and qualified professionals, and he emphasized the success of the Brazilian banking system, electronic voting, and income tax systems. These technological achievements impressed executives worldwide. With the combination of tax incentives and technological advancements, Jairo successfully convinced Dell to establish a software factory in Brazil.

After almost a year, at the end of 2001, Dell saw positive results from the Brazilian software factory and approved its expansion. The factory was initially located behind the computer factory in Eldorado do Sul, Rio Grande do Sul, but would now occupy an area of the Pontifical Catholic University (PUC-RS). Dell also decided to outsource some of its development work to a Brazilian company, presenting an opportunity for Stefanini.

This was Stefanini's chance to win a contract that would serve as an international showcase. Although they had previously secured contracts for software factories, this contract with Dell would be different. It would demonstrate Stefanini's global quality and reputation. To beat the competition, Stefanini needed to prove that they were one of the major national IT companies, which they had achieved with 300 active clients and revenues of BRL 85 million.

Additionally, they needed to have a local presence in Porto Alegre, which was a challenge as few Brazilian companies had successfully expanded nationwide. Thanks to the efforts of Bruno Mondin, Márcio Da Mata, and others, Stefanini had managed to establish nine branches in Brazil and open offices in Argentina, Mexico, Peru, Colombia, Chile, and the United States (although the US operations were still in their early stages and had few contracts).

In fact, at least in Brazil, there was no company with a greater presence than Stefanini. And one of the strongest branches was precisely the one in Porto Alegre, where Antonio Moreira worked, and it was consolidated with the acquisition of most of the RioSoft team.

The two attributes excluded the other five competitors, both the local ones in Porto Alegre, which were too small, and the large national ones, with no relevant presence in Rio Grande do Sul. Stefanini won that battle. Thanks to the national expansion started a few years prior, Marco won the chance to develop systems that would be used by a multinational corporation worldwide. As well as a contract for a software factory with a staff of 60.

Meanwhile, more than a year had passed since the opening of the branch in the United States, and Antonio was facing a strong headwind in the market. Smack in the middle of the crisis caused by the terrorist attack, there seemed to be no way for a Brazilian company to be taken seriously by IT executives in the United States. Plenty of phone calls, plane trips, and an enormous amount of time spent, all for barely any results. Some deals were made, but nothing major. In general, small, peripheral, and unprofitable services.

Late in the United States winter of 2002, Antonio discovered that Kimberly Clark, a giant in the consumer products industry, was starting a major implementation of the SAP management software. For an IT department, this is one of the most delicate moments possible. In a human body, it would be like replacing the entire nervous system at once, dealing with its ramifications in each limb (in this case, branches spread all over the world). Nobody hires an inexperienced supplier for such an operation. And Brazilians seemed to be all about sun and samba, not software.

The man who had to be convinced that this was not true, "the guy" to be found, was the American David Jacques, director of the global SAP project at Kimberly Clark. A senior executive who was constantly fawned upon by any global company, who received dozens of calls a week from companies around the world, eager to set up a simple meeting with an executive from such a corporation. Antonio needed to grab that man's attention. So, the branch secretary was instructed to call David as many times as necessary to get an appointment in his schedule. If Antonio were available, the secretary would transfer him the call so he could try to snatch an hour from the executive's schedule. If he were in a meeting, she would try to make the argument herself. It's an almost impossible task, known as a "cold call," trying to make an appointment with a top-level executive in the market without any prior relationship, reference, or consolidated brand.

And so it began. She would call once, twice, three times. And so she did in the afternoon again. Antonio would arrive at the branch and ask. - Nothing yet - the secretary said, shaking her head. Days went by, messages were left unanswered, and the man was always in a meeting or traveling or talking to the CEO. A week went by. In the second week, the attempts continued, though unsuccessfully. Time is of the essence in these cases. While a company tries to set up a simple meeting, others with prior relationships are already making proposals and putting figures on the table. That ocean liner had probably already sailed.

However, at the end of the third week, the unlikely thing happened. David Jacques had agreed to meet Antonio, a face-to-face encounter in the midst of an incredibly busy global executive schedule. That morning in late May, Antonio got on the plane to Atlanta, Kimberly Clark's headquarters.

He arrived ahead of time and was shown the sofa in the reception area. Antonio sat and waited. Thirty minutes after the scheduled meeting time, the eager Rio Grande do Sul native checked with the receptionist if David had already been notified. She nodded, but there was a sense that something was wrong. Another 15 minutes, 20 minutes, 40 minutes. Sixty minutes had passed since the scheduled time. The secretary called and said that there had been a problem with David's schedule and someone else was coming to see him.

Indeed, David Jacques himself came and apologized to Antonio, explaining that an unforeseen event had occurred and he would have to leave. But, of course, he could manage to talk for ten minutes:

"Look, I really can't stay any longer than that."

They entered a meeting room on the same floor, next to the reception, and Antonio quickly mentioned the names of the clients he had acquired in those two years (he listed them quickly, knowing that they were still small services). There wasn't even enough time to mention Dell, an asset at the time but of lesser importance in an SAP project.

Within those ten minutes, Antonio tried to show how Stefanini had experience in implementing management systems.

Across the table, David didn't look all that impressed. They had a great relationship with Deloitte, who could handle that part well. The eternal difficulty of beating an already established brand.

When David got up from his chair, worried about the time, Antonio played his last card:

"Have you already planned the first-tier service to support the implementation in Latin America?"

David paused for a moment as he considered the offer.

Seeing his way in, Antonio continued:

"You need a 'buffer' between users and the senior consulting team."

Antonio's proposal made sense. If the staff were bilingual, it would facilitate communication. And at a lower cost, because North American consultants were too "expensive" to stay on the phone fielding basic user questions.

David smiled and said:

"You're right."

Antonio shook David's hand and concluded:

"I will send you more information about this service, and we can set up another meeting when you get back."

Hours later, Antonio informed Marco about the lightning-fast meeting and began to elaborate a detailed proposal for how Stefanini could take care of the first-tier service (called TIER 1) during the SAP implementation process. He offered the most aggressive price he could, with as much detail as possible to ensure there would be no later changes, that this was a company with a track record and experience, despite the low price being offered.

The proposal was well received, and it looked like the first major contract would be won when David called Antonio and alerted that the fact that the company did not have a local office in Atlanta would be an issue, something difficult to ignore. The Deloitte consultancy was already carrying out SAP implementation for Kimberly Clark and had an office in the city, in addition to having a strong enough brand to charge a high price for its expertise.

Faced with the possibility of losing the contract, Antonio had no doubts:

"That's not a problem," he replied, willing to do anything to win over the service. "If we close this deal, Stefanini will open an office in the city to serve Kimberly Clark within one year, tops."

Stefanini won. It had no brand, but it was persistent and presented a detailed project. Two weeks later, two Brazilians arrived in Atlanta: a specialist in SAP and another to train the team with the methods used at Stefanini, an evolved version of the work developed by Carlos Henrique years before. Two Brazilians trained the local team of North Americans hired to carry out the work, two professionals who did not talk about samba or beer but rather about systems, methods, and management. With them, Stefanini taught North Americans the best way to carry out an information technology service. Six months after the contract was entered, Antonio opened its office in Atlanta.

The odyssey to arrange meetings and close deals happened hundreds of times in the first two years, often without a happy ending. Slowly, however, contracts were signed, and Antonio was able to establish references for Stefanini in the United States. The same strenuous work was carried out at all other branches that Marco opened worldwide. However, there was an opponent that put limits on their slow growth, an opponent that greatly reduced Stefanini's low-cost advantage. That opponent was India.

This situation could be compared to a battle where the situation seems to improve at the front, but a monumental attack erupts in the rear. On the one hand, the lack of a brand was the front, with Antonio and each branch's responsible person striving to assure that Stefanini could be relied upon. On the other hand, the competitive price, an advantage the Brazilians thought they had, was the rear. However, there was a much cheaper and well-known competitor: India.

Over the last few years, major Indian IT companies such as Tata, Infosys, and Wipro had been both an inspiration and a temptation for Brazilian companies. They made billions selling services in the United States market. While a beginner Brazilian programmer earned BRL 3,000, a young project leader in India earned less than half that amount. It didn't make sense to enter a fight with such low prices.

Price was just the most obvious aspect of the Indian competitor, who had multiple virtues and skills. Indian mathematicians had a long history of excellence, and their affinity for mathematics was deeply rooted. Furthermore, they spoke English fluently, which posed a challenge for Brazilian businesses interested in exporting and for those dealing with services where communication is key.

The Indian workforce had also significantly increased in numbers, with a population of 1.2 billion in 2011. Even though not all of them were proficient in English, there were still 320 million who were intimate with the language. This large English-speaking population presented a significant advantage for the Indian IT industry.

Indian companies made sure to showcase the quality of their services, similar to what Marco had done with the help of Carlos Henrique. They adhered to the best management practices defined in the Capability Maturity Model (CMM), a relatively unknown format at the time. The CMM became a recurring topic in every meeting Antonio attended in the United States, and potential clients would inquire if Stefanini had any level of CMM.

Realizing the importance of CMM, Antonio called Marco and said, "We need to go after our CMM." The first achievement was not so complicated because the processes had been organized six years earlier. In 2002, Stefanini obtained its level 2 CMM, becoming the third Brazilian company to earn this certification.

Just in time, because, at that same time, Dell's Indian branch was starting to bother and compete for projects with Dell Brazil. Two years after outsourcing the factory, Dell opened a second tender, not to potentially withdraw the contract from Stefanini but to divide that same service between two companies, which would compete against each other. Stefanini continued and gained a competitor. Pressure came from all sides.

The following year, the service would be divided between three companies. (A word of note: these companies that entered this second tender are no longer current suppliers at Dell in Porto Alegre, while Stefanini remains the main service provider for the North American computer giant.)

Did that mean the Indians were unbeatable, impossible to defeat? No. Well, perhaps in some cases. Antonio, Marco, and the rest of the market recognized that if the project consisted of a simple recipe and was restricted to coding, the Indian competition would win (this often happened with clients like Dell, who made this same consideration and increasingly sent projects for its Indian subsidiaries, in this case Dell India).

Let's dive a little deeper here. What does a "simple recipe" mean in an IT project? Imagine a system that programmers all over the world already know how to execute, something that has been produced millions of times and that just needs to be adapted to that specific company. Well, tell the Indians to receive the data like this, output it like that, and store it in this or that database. There's no reason to hire a first-class company, the usual North Americans or Europeans; simply hire whoever charges less for that job.

In simple cases like this, with projects lasting 10,000 hours, an Indian programmer costs USD 25 per hour, a Brazilian programmer costs up to USD 50, and an American programmer costs USD 90. Therefore, routine = India; quality = United States. So where does Brazil land in all of this?

The middle path that Antonio would have to follow would be to show that Brazilians had their qualities and virtues. In more complex cases, which required designing a specific solution, Brazil had an advantage. Indian professionals came from consulting companies in a country with scarce domestic industry. In Brazil, an infinity of factories, banks, and all kinds of segments created new, creative processes (national companies, such as Nitro Química, or branches of global firms, as was the case with Lloyds). And these professionals have true, everyday experience, the know-how of people who really know the rules of the trade.

If all it took was to define a discount policy, enter multiple promotions into the system, creatively analyze sales behavior, understand social concentration in a territory, or break the analysis down to a certain period of the month, well, the Indians didn't really know how to do that. This is a job for Brazilian developers and analysts (at the same time, Marco took care of strengthening the defense once again and, in 2005, Stefanini obtained its last CMM, level 5; it was the first Brazilian company to do so, whereas globally there were only 29 others with the same capability, mostly Indian and North American businesses).

So you have quality, creative flexibility, and a decent price. It seems quite obvious, perhaps even unimaginative marketing, but leaving no doubts was actually the point. But Brazil does not allow entrepreneurs to rest easy – it always offers a new opportunity to leave one's comfort zone. When Antonio thought he had found his pitch, the new push came in the form of an unstable and devalued exchange rate. In 2006, some of the factors that determined the creation of the factory in Rio Grande do Sul had changed. The Information Technology Law with the incentives that helped Jairo Avritchir convince the head offices was still in force, but the cost had increased enormously. The exchange rate at which USD 1 was worth BRL 3.2 was extremely advantageous; now, USD 1 was worth BRL 1.6. At the same time, competition from India had grown even stronger. Jairo knew that if he had to start the factory at that moment, in 2006, he wouldn't have been able – he would never have convinced the headquarters in Austin. Many projects were lost.

At the time, India maintained almost the same exchange rate and the same enviable price, earning 100 times more from IT services exports than Brazil. Let's see some figures: USD 36 billion against a timid USD 316 million raised by all companies on Brazilian soil (including not only national ones but also multinationals such as IBM, which represented most of this amount).

Marco knew that the competition that posed a real threat in the near future was not from Brazilian companies, but rather from the Indians. Indians were considered the Chinese of software and remote services, comparable to the unbeatable nature of the Chinese industry in manufacturing. Marco and Antonio saw an opportunity to join forces with the opponent and visited Dell's headquarters in Austin, Texas in mid-2006 to explore possibilities. In a conversation with the executive responsible for Dell's global development centers in India, Brazil, and Russia, they proposed the idea of opening a Stefanini branch in India. The response they received was positive, indicating that Dell would indeed do business with a development center in India.

By the end of 2006, Stefanini established itself in India, primarily to leverage the low production costs rather than to explore the local market. Today, the budget of Dell's Brazilian factory is twice the amount saved with tax exemptions, indicating that tax subsidies are no longer the main argument. The success lies in the quality and talent of Brazilian software, as well as Stefanini's ability to face international competition by utilizing Indian resources when necessary.

With a strong position in the market, Stefanini's revenues reached BRL 470 million, a significant amount for a Brazilian IT company that grew organically without external financial support. The company's global presence was recognized in rankings published by Fundação Dom Cabral, surpassing competitors in the IT sector. Stefanini's sales from abroad accounted for 20% of its total, mainly driven by contracts in the United States market.

However, Marco understood that further organic growth would be challenging, and competition would not wait for Stefanini to expand. He needed a new strategic move to surprise the market, whether it was selling outsourcing when it was not in demand, downsizing without prior experience, acquiring a bank's software factory, or achieving an important quality certification. Marco knew that North American, European, Indian, and Chinese companies were all aggressively vying for the Brazilian market. Moreover, the approaching economic crisis added to the uncertainty and challenges ahead, creating the potential for the end of an era.

CHAPTER 12

THE BEGINNING

Wall Street was on code red: it was game over for the Lehman Brothers Bank.

The alert was displayed on the TV screen, always turned on in the meeting room. Marco Stefanini stopped in his tracks, not knowing whether to sit down in his chair or turn up the volume on the news. The CNN presenter spoke, lips not making any sound, but the headline in the video left little room for doubt: after 158 years of existence and surviving two world wars, the crash of 1929 and September 11, the all-but-sacred Lehman Brothers was facing bankruptcy. This was no mere bank; Lehman Brothers was practically one of the pillars of the United States and global financial system. If the spinal cord were removed, the rest could very well fall with it.

Remote control in hand, Marco sat on the chair closest to the TV. CNN seemed to paint a dire picture – it made sense to get a second opinion from the BBC. On the British channel, the former chairman of the Federal Reserve (FED, the US Central Bank), Alan Greenspan, minimized the issue:

– We shouldn't try to protect each and every institution –, the finance wizard said. – There are winners and losers at any game –, Greenspan calmly declared, his air of superiority all the more pronounced as he adjusted his square-rimmed glasses with one hand.

For many, the US government had gone too far. Six months earlier, in March 2008, the Federal Reserve bailed out Bear Stearns, America's fifth largest investment bank. That was good fortune for J.P. Morgan, which paid USD 2 per share, whereas the price two days earlier was still close to USD 30. All of that with a USD 30 billion "father to son" loan from the FED. At the time, the collapse of the super-bank shook the market, and Marco decided to indefinitely postpone the IPO of Stefanini IT Solutions.

In early September 2008, the time came for real estate finance companies Fannie Mae and Freddie Mac. In this case, the US government ended up buying the bankrupt companies for USD 200 billion.

All of that outlined a gloomy prognosis for the global economy. It also felt like a bottomless pit. On the same Sunday that Barclays pulled out of Lehman, Bank of America bought Merrill Lynch, albeit at less than half the price it cost a year earlier. Some relief came from that. Perhaps it was time to shut down the corporate hospital and let Lehman Brothers go down on its own. But whatever decision was made in the United States, that crisis could be the biggest of all time.

Marco got up from the couch and picked up his cell phone. It was mid-afternoon on Sunday, September 14th. Time to call Stefanini's top echelon. If the world was going to end, they better be prepared for it. He called and wrote e-mails to the twenty executives, warning that a conference call would be held the next day, Monday, at 8:00 am. What Marco said to them would then be disseminated to Stefanini's more than seven thousand employees.

The next day, when it was time for the meeting, Marco was straight to the point.

– We need two things: to sell more and to find alternatives for the crisis.

Stefanini needed to move faster; however, it was also imperative to create new offerings, to provide options to the upwards of 300 corporations they served. It was also high time to win over other clients. Marco thought that the crisis could be his chance to get ahead of the game. It had happened before; crises could be a good thing. The meeting ended, the executives got up, and Marco remembered that he hadn't said anything about cutting costs. "That's alright," he thought, "I don't think we have to talk about that now. What matters is that we act quickly."

Indeed, the urgency was there. That same week, clients started calling in attempts to suspend or renegotiate contracts; Brazil was scared. Nevertheless, the start of the crisis was good for Stefanini. Marco knew that, at the tail end of 2008, there was still time to race and close some deals, since many companies had a budget then that would probably be smaller the following year. And that's how the year 2008 ended well. But nothing would be like that from then on.

And it wasn't just Brazil that got scared: the whole world was frightened. Not only had the Americans allowed Lehman Brothers to fail, but in September Congress rejected US Treasury Secretary Henry Paulson's economic rescue plan. In October 2008, the Financial Times warned that the crisis would be much worse than in 1997 (which sounded fine, Stefanini didn't even face any hardships in 1997).

But the century-old British newspaper compared the problem to the 1987 crisis - in both cases, the market imploded on a Black Monday, sure, but now the bankruptcy of the global credit system was announced, and it no longer had anything to do with the oil shock. Maybe it wouldn't be so bad; after all, it was in the midst of the 1987 crisis that Marco officially opened

Stefanini. But the newspaper went further: the current crisis could become as catastrophic as the economic disaster of 1929. The global financial system itself was in serious danger of falling apart. After that, nobody knew what could happen.

In Brazil, in early October, the reaction was conservative; President Lula ordered the Minister of Finance, Guido Mantega, to spare the Central Bank's reserves. Thus, in less than 48 hours, the dollar jumped from BRL 2.19 to BRL 2.45. In the following week, almost BRL 40 billion left smaller banks for the bigger ones in search of security. The threat of the collapse of the financial system was approaching Brazil.

In December, speculators bet against the real, and Mantega was forced to open the coffers when the dollar reached BRL 2.62. The losers in this bet were the financial directors of major corporations, such as Aracruz and Sadia, who saw billions of reais evaporate in investments with derivatives that were excessively risky.

The difference between the 1987 crisis and the current one was that, before, the stock market suffered, but the real economy was barely affected (at least in the United States; in Brazil, we know that the crisis hit much harder: as usual, when the United States catches a cold, Brazil suffers a major bout of the flu). This time, the origin of the crisis was credit, and from there, it ricocheted into consumption and investment.

The butterfly's wings were flapping and creating a hurricane. To make things clear, the origin of the famous metaphor placed the butterfly in Brazil, not in Asia. In 1972, mathematician and meteorologist Edward Lorenz rhetorically asked: "Does the flapping of a butterfly's wings in Brazil cause a hurricane in Texas?" In the following years, the metaphor was used extensively to show how the global system was interconnected.

For us, usually, the wings flapped over there, while we were tormented over here.

Due to this same speed factor, there was also the hope that, contrary to what happened in 1929, the reaction of the global authorities would be faster. The financial system was a cipher; it took the hit broadly and faster, but it could also bounce back more easily. The future was uncertain.

The avalanche of bad news was so great that it didn't just affect customers; it also had the power to hurt the morale of Stefanini's own employees. Marco knew that he had to convey to his employees the certainty that no crisis had ever hindered Stefanini in those 21 years. The company was coming of age, and the crises so far had only helped the company grow (he hoped it would be the same this time around).

The entrepreneur suspected that this message would weaken if it were transmitted from the top echelon to the managers, from the managers to analysts and consultants in the cells, and from there to each programmer. He needed to speak directly to every Stefanini employee.

These were Marco's thoughts after leaving a meeting with his top executives. It was barely past noon, and he was very hungry. He thought about having lunch but gave up on the idea. It was critical that employees get the message as soon as possible.

He clicked on the message icon, selected the All option, and watched the cursor blink. What could he say to show employees that there was no need to fear the crisis, quite the opposite, in fact? Facts. Stefanini's history spoke for itself. And then he started typing:

> Team Stefanini, this is an important announcement:
> In our successful history, Stefanini has always overcome challenges and achieved success in

times of crisis. At the end of these difficult periods, we have emerged with much more positive results than when we entered.

"Perfect, this is it", he thought. We have to do what we did before. Now I need to reinforce what we must do today.

And this time, we are going to increasingly focus our efforts, maintaining the same drive and energy, so that we have increasingly pleasing results!

– Great, this is essential. But I also need to remind them of our advantages. If they remember that we are better, this will clarify why we manage to win contracts while others lose. So I'll start with a rhetorical question:

Why does Stefanini offer better and more advantageous conditions than all our competitors?

Let's start with the irrefutable facts:

Greater number of clients (more diversified base) - we have virtually all major banks, telecom, and insurance companies as active clients. Most major industrial companies, energy, and Oil & Gas are also our clients. Our earnings are not concentrated among a few customers.

Next, the obvious:

Trusting, long-term relationships with clients.

And now, something unique to us:

The company has solid financial liquidity and does not have any debt on the market. Our growth is continuous, with a well-balanced financial situation. In times like these, these factors are worth gold!

Now, let's remind ourselves of who we are and ask for everyone's help:

We have established command structures and teams staffed with competent and capable people who can take whatever measures are needed to solve the situation.

It is crucial that we rely on all employees at this critical time.

However, let's be more specific about what Stefanini needs right now, so it is clear what we can do. If I ask for help, you may wonder how. Here's what we expect:

a) Maintain high-quality service, as satisfied customers are less likely to discontinue services.

b) Pay attention to opportunities and notify salespeople (managers, officers, the VP, and myself) so that we can take advantage of these opportunities, including advancing on the services of our competitors.

Great, this is what I wanted to convey: that the crisis is the perfect opportunity to gain territory rather than lose it. But let's not forget to mention what we, as a company, are doing. We are not standing idly in the face of the crisis, and your contributions are not the only ones.

Here's what Stefanini is doing:

More aggressive marketing - with the "Performance Leader" campaign, we are going to show the market that Stefanini is the safest IT provider.

Strong cost control on all expenses.

Improved customer service - we count on all employees in these efforts.

Understanding our clients and their needs, looking for alternative solutions. What can we do to help? How can we increase revenue? How can we reduce our clients' costs?

Reducing costs is important; it is always helpful if everyone makes small suggestions. I didn't mention that at the meeting, but I believe it would be better for them to focus on increasing sales rather than solely emphasizing cost-cutting efforts. Additionally, I am unsure whether I should raise the topic of acquisitions here. Up to this point, we have been unsuccessful in acquiring any significant international company, despite discussing it since 2007. Nevertheless, I will bring up this point to demonstrate that the subject has not been overlooked. Finally, I would like to conclude with words of encouragement:

Continuing with the acquisition program – looking for new and worthwhile opportunities; and

Working hard to come out of this crisis stronger than when we came in!

Moving full speed ahead, that's our challenge!

I wish you all an excellent week,

Marco Stefanini

– Excellent, I think that will do. Oops, I forgot the subject. That's easy, it'll be my motto:

SUBJECT: Stefanini – for us, crises are synonymous with opportunity!

This wasn't Marco's first email to all of his employees, but it was the most comprehensive in a long time, the most sure-fire message in a crisis, and the one that reached the most people. After all, that email would reach five thousand employees before they left for lunch.

Of course, it wouldn't be the last message either. From then on, emails became the quickest way to communicate to Stefanini employees what was truly happening in that economic crisis, a way to counterbalance the catastrophic news one would read and hear about in the media. Marco wanted his employees to see the economic crisis from his perspective, as well as from the perspective of other people who also inspired him.

For instance, in mid-November, Marco wrote everyone recalling what Sam Walton, the founder of Walmart, had said about the 1991 recession (the one Marco used to turn Stefanini around and enter the outsourcing market). Walton said:

– They asked what I thought of the recession. I've thought about it and decided not to participate.

The quote translated Marco's thoughts to a tee. At the end of the email, he made a note saying that, in spite of the crisis, Stefanini had grown in October.

Ten days later, it was time to use a quote from businessman Jorge Gerdau. He and Marco were colleagues at the CEO Forum, an annual event that both attended, and where they had already met presidents Lula and George W. Bush, and where, the following year, they would meet Barack Obama.

Gerdau's quote was as follows:

– I like crises. It is in crises that we learn to work better and more efficiently.

He continued:

– We have always come out of a crisis much better and stronger than when we came in.

The phrase wasn't Marco's, but he couldn't think of anything that better expressed his thinking, the way he had led Stefanini since the first crisis.

There were new elements to this scenario, concerns that Marco had not considered in the other crises. Not just because Stefanini was now earning almost BRL 500 million, and the higher the climb, the higher the fall. But also because the crisis ruined plans Marco had cooked for a long time. Plans that had been divulged countless times in press releases, plans he'd talked about in hundreds of interviews with journalists, and now...

The first and most hindered of the plans would be Stefanini's entry into the stock market. The practice known in stock exchange parlance as an "IPO" – or initial public offering.

There are many reasons for a company to offer its capital in the market. The most obvious is to get money for cheap. However, the most impressive effect – which became known to the general population – was to create billionaire entrepreneurs overnight, a process even more intense in the phenomenon of Internet companies, in which young people in t-shirts and ripped jeans became extremely wealthy. Marco was no longer a young man, approaching the age of 50, but he would have good use and investment for the capital obtained from the stock.

Another excellent reason for making Stefanini go public was to increase confidence among clients. A publicly traded company conveys more security to the market, especially to clients. There are many ways to do this, like being a global company, which Stefanini was already doing, but they still had a long way to go. Going public could help in several ways.

All over Brazil, entrepreneurs thought exactly like Marco. In the previous year alone, in 2007, there were 64 IPOs in Brazil – two of them ranked among the 10 largest in the world in terms of amounts raised. Billions of reais were earned in the operations.

Marco had spent the last few years preparing Stefanini for this moment. He made the company a corporation, rigorously published perfect balance sheets, went over the company with a fine-tooth comb. All to get to the IPO pot.

In November 2007, Marco announced that the IPO would finally take place in the second quarter of 2008. However, he did not anticipate the major crisis that was approaching at the beginning of the year. As a result, he had to revise his prediction, and the new projected date for the IPO was between September and October of 2008, hoping for a better market environment. Unfortunately, in that year, only 13 companies dared to go public, and 7 of them raised less than their initial plans.

When the scheduled date arrived, the market conditions were still unfavorable, leading to another postponement of the IPO. Eventually, in March 2009, Marco decided to give up on the IPO project indefinitely and announced it to the market. Although some companies managed to go public in 2009, even in the technology sector and similar in size to Stefanini, the outcomes were poor and fell below expectations. Stefanini had to proceed with its expansion plans without the IPO, considering the possibility of revisiting the idea when the market improved and the company had grown further.

The challenges and delays faced with the IPO also influenced another of Marco's intentions, which was widely discussed in press interviews: the acquisition of an IT company in the United States. The United States market was resistant to the idea of buying IT services from Brazilian companies, as observed by Antonio Moreira from Stefanini USA. While the international branches had brought experience and good contracts over almost ten years of operation, Marco realized that waiting for Stefanini to reach the same size in Brazil would take too long, and it still wouldn't be enough to compete with expanding Indian companies. Time was of the essence.

The alternative path forward was something Marco had never done before: acquiring a large company in the international market. This approach was being adopted by businesspeople across various sectors. In 2004 alone, Brazilians spent USD 6.64 billion on acquisitions abroad. Notable cases included AmBev's merger with the Belgian company Interbrew in 2004, forming InBev, and later acquiring the American brewing icon, Anheuser-Busch. Gerdau, the steel company, also made numerous acquisitions in countries such as Peru, Spain, Mexico, Venezuela, Colombia, Argentina, and primarily the United States. These ventures helped transform the Brazilian brand into something that extended beyond soccer and samba.

Since 2007, Marco had been publicly expressing his interest in acquiring businesses abroad. However, he gradually realized that buying a quality asset at a favorable price was much more challenging than he had anticipated. Meanwhile, his competitors in Brazil were finding their own paths to navigate the market. For example, Politec from Brasilia sold 10% of the company to the Japanese group Mitsubishi, which allowed them to capitalize, demonstrate solidity, and expand into the international market.

This was not an option for Marco, who neither wanted nor thought it necessary to sell the company, now that it had grown so much, earned the respect of the market, and opened so many branches abroad.

The problem is that, by the end of 2007, Marco had already evaluated 20 companies. And no acquisition had taken place.

Since the process did not seem to move forward, he decided to give Antonio Barretto, the man he had hired to coordinate the IPO, the task of coordinating the acquisitions (we must not mistake this Antonio who handled IPOs and acquisitions with Antonio Moreira from Stefanini USA). When the IPO project was aborted three months later, buying companies became Barretto's main task.

And he knew how to evaluate them. For four years, he worked at Votorantim's financial department, first as an executive in Brazil, then as vice president of a division in the United States. Therefore, he also had extensive international experience. Moreover, Barretto was tech-savvy, having worked ten years earlier at Canadian telecommunications equipment manufacturer Nortel Networks. All things considered, he was the right person for the job.

In early 2008, when he arrived, Barretto asked for the list of 20 companies to come to understand what had already been evaluated. For a year, Barretto would carefully evaluate dozens of potential targets, mainly in the United States market. The global chaos and the currency debacle did not help him at all. The value of companies fell, and the owners refused to hand over the company they had founded for an amount that much lower than what they thought it was worth.

At the end of 2008, the exchange rate seesaw worsened the scenario. From BRL 1.56 in July, the dollar soared to BRL 2.33

at the end of the year. The acquisition cost increased, making Marco rethink the entire transaction.

At that time, a company in the US state of Michigan was going through a crucial period. During the weeks following the outbreak of the North American crisis, board members would meet in an attempt to define the best course of action.

The company was called TechTeam and was located in Southfield, right in the heart of the American crisis. An explanation is in order: Southfield is part of the greater metropolis of Detroit. In a process similar to that of the ABC region in São Paulo, Brazil, the United States automobile hub witnessed the gradual escape of factories during the previous decade, causing constant and irrecoverable decay. When the 2008 crisis arrived, it was the last straw. And the straw broke.

In the region, one could buy a house for USD 6,000. With the crisis, the state achieved the unenviable position of having the highest unemployment rate in the United States.

TechTeam, along with several clients in the automotive industry – and many others who also felt the effects of the crisis – had few options. It also faced competition from the Indians and needed to keep expanding, but it did not have access to credit sources (like all US companies at that time).

This was the dilemma discussed consecutively by TechTeam board members between late September and early November. At the end of that period, the board members decided that they could sell one of the two divisions of the IT services company. One provided services to private sector companies, the other to the government. The board members thought of selling the latter.

At that same time, by the end of November 2008, a TechTeam executive made contact with Stefanini. The proposal was to form a partnership in the North American projects at Portuguese-speaking markets.

The following month, Antonio (Moreira, from the North American branch, not Barretto) flew to Detroit to meet the executives and discuss the idea. He liked what he saw and later commented to Marco that TechTeam could be an excellent acquisition in the United States. Five days later, the Americans received an anonymous letter – which used an office as an intermediary – revealing a company's interest in acquiring TechTeam.

The recipient of the letter was Gary Cotshott, President and CEO of TechTeam. He was part of the group of board members, led by Seth Hamot, who discussed, since the start of the crisis, the hardships of pursuing any strategy with the credit crunch in the international market. In late February, as the crisis deepened, Seth and the other board members began to discuss the possibility of selling TechTeam entirely.

At that time, on March 19, 2009, Marco and Antonio Moreira took a plane and went to meet the company's directors in New York. Marco thought his search was over. TechTeam was strong in support services (service desk) and business process outsourcing (BPO). In total, it employed 2,400 people. It would be a relevant acquisition, consolidating Stefanini's presence in the United States market. Marco became frustrated: Gary Cotshott said TechTeam was not for sale.

Back in Brazil, Marco found himself facing more everyday problems. Now the crisis was hitting the domestic market hard. Even the population could feel it. At the beginning of 2009, the unemployment rate hit a record-breaking level, surpassed only by the 1984 index, the same one that made Marco suffer so much when looking for a job after graduating as a geologist from USP.

Unemployment figures from the bitter past were coming back at a bad time.

Inside Stefanini, the crisis was felt in the profit margins, which had fallen sharply. The crisis had reached the company and something had to be done. Merely chasing new businesses wasn't going to cut it. They had to look inside the company and then start cutting. To the bone.

Marco wasn't thinking about firing anyone at that time. However, adjustments needed to be made. In December, he wrote another one of his emails to all employees. This time, the key word was COST:

– It's like a nail, you always have to cut it; there is no irreducible cost; cutting can be spontaneous or compulsory; if we don't cut ourselves down, our competitors will instead.

The message couldn't be any clearer. Either cut down or die.

This notion came in time, but it was still late. The months of January and February of 2009 were bad for Stefanini. In the following months, Marco would look carefully at each client, squeezing those who, due to specific problems, were making a loss instead of a profit. No matter how well done a project is, there is always a great chance that it will not go as planned. Stefanini's methods certainly reduced the margin of error, but there is no way to eliminate it. At that moment, however, it would not be possible to tolerate mistakes because the good cells no longer compensated for the damage caused by the bad ones. Almost 30 cells still posted negative results and began to undergo constant monitoring.

In June, things started to improve somewhat. For every client who called during the crisis to suspend or reduce a project, the managers would make an irresistible counter-proposal – instead of reducing, increase our services, and you won't pay any extra for it. Negotiations were tough, but after eight months of crisis, not a single client had canceled any projects. Better yet: Petrobras had sped up operations with its partner IBM, had increased, and Mônica had made significant advances in several projects in São Paulo and in the local branches. A decent contract was entered with the automaker Fiat, and the Caixa Econômica service, won in 2008, went live in the middle of the year. Even better: while competitors lost contracts and clients because the losses were too great, Stefanini increased its market share further, taking on hundreds of employees at a price good enough to be an interesting deal for both sides. Stefanini breathed and grew during the crisis.

As a sign of improvement in the market, Visa went public, in one of the longest processes of its kind (it took four years). It was worth it; the IPO raised BRL 8.4 billion and exceeded the IPO of oil explorer OGX, with BRL 6.6 billion. Visa was the biggest IPO in the history of the Brazilian stock market. Still not enough to make Marco change his mind about taking Stefanini public, but an excellent indicator of improvements in the market and of the world's interest in Brazil.

The following month, Marco took a plane to Washington for the fourth meeting of the Brazil-United States CEO Forum. Basically, it was an event in which ten presidents of Brazilian companies met with ten from North American companies. Government ministers and senior officials from both countries were also at the table. The original purpose was to discuss topics of interest to both sides, in particular a way to reduce double taxation (those who do business between the two countries end up paying tax twice on the same service or product). On other occasions, Marco had the opportunity to meet George W. Bush, then-minister Dilma Rousseff, and President Lula. Now, he was hoping to meet Barack Obama.

Moreover, this time the meeting would take place on US soil. On the first day of the event, Monday, July 20, Marco called Miguel Jorge, then Minister of Development, Industry, and Trade. He had a proposal, something that should benefit the country and at the same time help Stefanini in the long term with one of its main difficulties: finding qualified professionals.

Hiring and keeping good programmers and analysts had always been an obstacle. Ever since Márcio Da Mata approached programmers at USP to assemble the Bamerindus team, or when Mônica and Aparecida had to run to prevent the Lloyds team from disappearing out of thin air, the search for qualified people in Brazil had always been a major hindrance.

At a previous event, Marco had heard from Alcoa's global president, Alain Belda, the idea of using tax incentives in the educational area. At the time, Marco liked what he heard and took the idea to the then Chief of Staff, Dilma Rousseff, who was also attending the meeting. She took kindly to the idea, and Marco's next step would be to present it to the Minister of Development, Industry, and Trade. Now was the time.

Marco had good expectations that Minister Miguel Jorge would like the idea since he knew that the Minister agreed with the need to invest in education, that without it, Brazil would never be the country of the present: we would always be looking to a future that would never arrive. This was his proposal: companies that invested in educational entities would be able to deduct income tax expenses. A sort of Rouanet Law (Brazil's renowned culture incentive law), but for education.

The minister took a good look at Marco and said that it could really make a difference. Once the idea was approved, Miguel Jorge would take the document so that the ministry could develop a draft bill that would be presented to Congress. The text was developed and is now waiting to be presented once again to Dilma Rousseff, now President of the Republic.

***

During his trip back to Brazil, at the end of July 2009, Marco thought more than ever about the need to grow in the United States market. Just as with the IPO project, the businessman had a fixed idea in mind: buying a company that would allow Stefanini to expand its operations in the United States and the world once and for all.

This movement was unlike anything else Marco had done in Stefanini's 22-year history. Until then, the company had followed its course, from zero to BRL 500 million, without buying any competitor, always with organic growth. But Marco couldn't count on another twenty years to grow abroad. The competition was moving forward.

The day after the event, when Marco was already back in Brazil, an important event took place in Southfield, Detroit. An undisclosed company, known to be one of Stefanini's global competitors, made an offer at USD 116 million to buy all of TechTeam, both the private and government-serving divisions. The offer was made because the board had now officially divulged its intentions of selling the company. Ultimately, the company ended up relinquishing the purchase, but the board's decision was clear. TechTeam was on the market.

In recent months, despite Marco's disappointment at the New York meeting, Barretto continued to stay in touch with TechTeam representatives. The CEO himself, Gary Cotshott, had given the message that the company would be open to receiving offers from Stefanini. For him, no prospective buyer should be left aside. Over the next six months, TechTeam reached out to 97 companies and investors. From this set, 62 actually signed nondisclosure agreements to receive sensitive information related to the government division.

Stefanini was one of the first to do so. However, in a conference call held on May 12, Barretto himself made it clear that he was only interested in buying the entire company, and that, after the acquisition, they were going to sell the government division. In June, shortly before going to the CEO Forum, Stefanini had made an offer at USD 77.9 million.

The great problem in selling the government division was that one of the main customers was the US Department of Defense. The US government could delay and disrupt the transaction if the buyer were foreign. The proposals offered by Stefanini and the unknown competitor did not explain what would be done if that happened.

In early August 2009, Marco and Barretto decided that the best thing to do would be to simply give up on buying the government division. Stefanini offered USD 48 million for the division focused on the private sector. The portion that served the government was no longer of interest.

Until that moment, Seth Hamot and the directors had been disappointed with the values offered for the separate divisions, somewhere between USD 40 million and USD 60 million. And Stefanini, since it was lowballing, was considered the underdog of the race, mainly because it no longer showed any interest in the government division. Seth sent word that the offer devalued TechTeam and that he had expected better. Marco thought it best to not do so (he would later regret it). Based on the offers placed on the table, the directors decided to suspend the sale process once again. It was just not enough money.

On October 15, Barretto submitted a new offer: USD 67.9 million. No reply came back. In November, Marco and Antonio asked for a meeting to discuss the proposal and, perhaps, increase the amount. They took a plane and went to meet the TechTeam directors in New York.

For an hour, he and Antonio listened to the chairman of the board, Seth Hamot, give an extensive description of what TechTeam was all about: the number of employees, the customers, the branches abroad, especially in Europe. After the lengthy presentation, Marco briefly spoke about Stefanini and got straight to the point: "I want to buy your business."

Neither Marco nor Antonio could foresee what would happen next. Perhaps Seth figured he could find a buyer for the government division, maybe he thought the government could provide more aid to major clients like Ford and GM and that things would get better for TechTeam. No one knows for certain. The truth is that Seth said:

– Sorry, TechTeam is not for sale.

For someone who traveled 10,000 kilometers because they thought they had found what they were looking for more than three years, hearing something like that can be very frustrating. Marco couldn't believe his ears, and, in disbelief, he slowly got up and walked over to the cookie table. While Marco turned his back on the directors, Seth continued talking, now only looking at Antonio, about the partnership possibilities that TechTeam and Stefanini could explore. Meanwhile, still with his back turned to Seth, Marco slowly filled his glass with orange juice, thinking about the time he had lost and the search that would have to continue, about how an executive could possibly signal and negotiate the sale of a company and then simply state: "TechTeam is not for sale."

Marco came back to his chair and interrupted Seth:

– Sorry, but I think we've all wasted time here. You wasted it talking to us and I wasted it leaving Brazil to talk to you.

He got up, said goodbye and left the room.

For several months, the TechTeam issue was gradually forgotten at Stefanini. However, in February 2010, a company that had already shown interest in the acquisition, Jacobs Engineering, came back to discuss the purchase of the government division. Almost five months later, Jacobs and TechTeam divulged an agreement for the sale of the government division to the market.

TechTeam got what it had always wanted, capitalizing on the USD 59 million paid by Jacobs. At that time, the directors could take the money and carry out their original plan to invest in the company. The thing is, now the strategy had changed; they knew that money alone would not solve their situation, and they also knew that TechTeam needed to be part of a larger group, something that would allow them to stand up to the competition.

The situation was similar to Stefanini's, with the aggravating factor that TechTeam depended heavily on the United States market, which was stagnant and facing a crisis, while Stefanini continued to be capitalized and was in one of the strongest markets during that crisis. The board remained willing to sell the commercial division as well. And, in July, Stefanini made a new offer, worth USD 73 million. The directors remained silent.

Days passed, and Marco knew that at any moment another company could take TechTeam away from him – just a few million dollars more and the directors would be swayed. In late October, he authorized Barretto to make a final bid of USD 94 million for TechTeam's private division.

The answer came on November 2nd. After being notified by the board, Barretto went to meet Marco at a lunch with Stefanini's board members. He came closer and said, without being overheard:

– It worked.

For the rest of the afternoon, Barretto brought documents for Marco to sign, under the suspicious gaze of all the Stefanini managers. The mystery was required because the battle was not yet won.

TechTeam was a publicly traded company, with almost all of its capital held by market shareholders. Of course, board approval was still important, mainly for two reasons: because it included major shareholders and because they would be heard by the other shareholders. But convincing the board was merely the first part of the challenge.

Ten days after the board of directors' reply, Stefanini published an ad in a major US newspaper notifying the market that an offer had been made to TechTeam shareholders. From that point forward, they had until December 10th to accept or reject that offer.

On November 19, the deadline approached, and only 18.39% of the shares were held by Stefanini. There were twenty days left. Marco needed to buy 50% of the shares plus one to be able to control the company. Without being able to control its operations, there would be no advantage in owning shares in a company. And even the smallest percentage of control could still not be the best deal because acquiring the rest could take time and cost more than anticipated.

One more week, and the number reached 18.54%. Four more days, and progress was still slight, at only 21.64%. There were ten days left. After a long process, negotiations, travels, and offers, that acquisition could still go wrong. Marco could visualize TechTeam getting away from him.

Three days before the deadline, Barretto called Marco and notified him: Stefanini now owned 51.08% of TechTeam. It was official: they were in control.

On December 10, the deadline for shareholders to accept the offer, the number of shares acquired reached 89.36%. After almost five years looking to make acquisitions and going back and forth on the negotiation table, Stefanini had transformed itself into a company with a true presence in the United States market, with important operations in other countries. Furthermore, Stefanini IT Solutions directly reached 27 countries and employed 12,000 people. Its annual revenue exceeded BRL 1 billion. All in the midst of a crisis.

Human beings' desire to exceed their own limits seems to have an intimate relationship with hardships. This can become explicit in the strange relationship between the tallest buildings in the world and the worst crises. Right after the historic crisis of 1929, the construction of the Empire State Building began. Further evidence of this trend: the year after World War II, plans began for another skyscraper, the World Trade Center. The project was halted, to be completed on the eve of the 1973 oil shock. It was destroyed by terrorists in 2001, with a new set of towers being built over the next decade. Recently, by the end of this economic crisis, the world record was once again beaten by the Burj Khalifa skyscraper, measuring 828 meters, in the emerging power of Dubai. In crises, the entrepreneurial spirit wishes to fly even higher.

In 2010, Stefanini was not the only company to build its corporate skyscraper and make history. Days before acquiring TechTeam, the steelmaker Gerdau paid USD 1.6 billion for the shares it did not yet hold in the United States company Ameristeel. Shortly before that, the meatpacking company Marfrig bought Keystone, also from the United States, for USD 1.26 billion. Green-and-yellow multinationals took advantage of Brazil's strong currency to go shopping.

155

However, not to diminish the importance of Marfrig and Gerdau, Stefanini's acquisition was particularly historic, marking a unique event for Brazil. It was the first time a Brazilian company in the technology sector had acquired a major brand in the United States market. In 2011, after acquiring TechTeam, Stefanini's new ranking by Fundação Dom Cabral sent a clear message: it was now the second-ranked among all internationalized Brazilian companies, only outranked by JBS-Friboi.

Moreover, Stefanini, which had started from scratch in a small room on Avenida Paulista and had never undergone a merger or major acquisition before, managed to achieve annual revenues of over BRL 1 billion. This accomplishment was even more remarkable considering it took place during one of the most severe economic crises in the history of global capitalism. It was a symbolic achievement, showcasing that Stefanini was created and developed amidst crises.

While Stefanini was solidifying its position, older and larger competitors were being acquired by international capital, including the French, North Americans, Spanish, Portuguese, and Chileans. At the same time, Stefanini's growth propelled it to become six times larger than the second-largest Brazilian company in terms of capital.

Following the bankruptcy of Lehman Brothers, the crisis persisted, albeit to a lesser extent, in rich countries. Among the emerging countries, Russia experienced a recession, while China and India faced a dip in growth. In the group known as BRIC (Brazil, Russia, India, and China), Brazil was the least affected, at least until the end of 2010. The local sentiment was still one of hope, with the expectation that the long-dreamed country of the future could finally become a reality. The GDP had grown by

7.5%, and unemployment was below 7%, nearing what economists refer to as "full employment."

However, the scenario would soon change. This reversal of expectations wouldn't be the greatest adversity for a company accustomed to navigating economic crises. The next major challenge for Stefanini would be to consolidate its company's identity, integrating the acquired branches and transmitting its culture to them. With its newfound global presence, Stefanini would have to successfully navigate this challenge.

CHAPTER 13

INTEGRATION

D espite the shining sun, the thermometer indicated minus 10 degrees Celsius. Marco stamped his feet, unsuccessfully trying to warm himself up. They were in front of TechTeam's headquarters, in a building located in the city of Southfield, part of the greater Detroit metropolitan area, in the US state of Michigan. In front of the building, three flags stood tall: one for Brazil, one for the United States, and the Michigan State Flag. Over the next few hours, during the visit, Marco would meet a few hundred Americans.

They were the human face of the recession that had officially ended in 2009. One of the many effects of the crisis had been the sale of United States companies to foreigners. Stefanini and TechTeam's case was far from unique. And each employee of the acquired company feared for their future.

To each employee he met, Marco would repeat: "How are you?" Throughout his life, he had paid little attention to English lessons. He even studied at a nationally known network of schools, Cultura Inglesa, but Brazil was not all that open a culture, and learning a foreign language was not considered as important as it is today. The situation would later change, but he never did have time to start studying again. This, however, did not stop him from attempting to communicate. "I'll have to make do with my spaghetti English," he thought.

"How are you?" he kept repeating while greeting the employees.

At that time, language was not a cause for concern. Upon acquiring the company, Stefanini faced the most difficult and frequent dilemma in situations like that: changing the culture. On the one hand, it was always reasonable to imagine that there was something to improve in a company that had suffered from the economic crisis. After all, Stefanini not only survived but thrived.

Walking around the office, Marco noticed that several rooms were closed down. TechTeam still employed the classic model, in which each executive had their own sequestered office in which to carry out their work, with sparse interactions within the team. Stefanini had abandoned this model decades before when everyone started to work side by side, in the same environment. Even top executives were not isolated in individual rooms but shared the same space together.

On the other hand, Marco was perfectly aware that it was neither possible nor desirable to arrive at a company and raze its original culture to the ground. In every country, there are customs and practices that must be respected and, in most cases, appreciated. This was one of the core mistakes made by foreign companies, as in the case of the Chinese businesses that acquired American operations, ignoring local singularities. Years later, the American Factory documentary would show the problems of this culture clash, portraying the hardships of a Chinese company when acquiring a business in the American state of Ohio. The film was even awarded an Oscar.

However, in that year of 2010, Marco only had the intuition that the best course of action was to proceed with caution and respect. Mainly because every change process already faces resistance in normal situations, a fact indicated in academic research and that Marco himself was able to witness in practice over the years. When questioned, the overwhelming majority of those involved are in favor of innovating, as long as there are no radical changes in their own sector. When these changes occur, one of the methods of opposition can be described as "passive resistance."

In these cases, employees restrict themselves to doing only what is ordered or even verbally agreed upon, but without carrying out given tasks. In some cases, they may also withhold information, feign ignorance, reduce the work pace, and increase their absenteeism levels. This would be one of the main challenges in the following years.

Two months after visiting TechTeam's former headquarters in Michigan, Stefanini set up the 2011 kick-off, an annual event that welcomed executives from all Stefanini operations around the world. It was the sixth event of its kind but the first after the TechTeam acquisition, when it was possible to understand what it meant for the company's future. The event began on Wednesday, February 9, at the Bourbon Ibirapuera Hotel, with the day ending in a dinner party for executives, where there was a unique sight to behold.

Dozens of foreign executives shared the table with their Brazilian counterparts. Twenty-nine people came from the United States, including Brazilians and Americans. From Europe, twenty-two, and from Latin America, thirty. There were also two people from Asia: an executive from China and an American who was working at the TechTeam branch in Manila, Philippines. English and Portuguese sentences mingled in the air, and several words could occasionally be heard in other languages. Few scenes could have been more representative of what Stefanini had become, a visual portrayal of a company that now spanned 27 countries around the world.

Everyone was there in an attempt to understand what it meant to be part of a Brazilian technology company. Many executives feared they would not be able to integrate. As a reference, many remembered a scene that entered the discourse on major acquisitions, one which took place in 2004 when Ambev acquired the Belgian company InterBrew. When presenting their remuneration system to the employees of the Belgian branch, the latter began to get up, one by one, and leave the room. Before the presentation ended, only the Brazilians remained.

Other companies made a preemptive strike after an acquisition, preferring to do a "clean house," dismissing local executives and replacing the entire top echelon with people of the nationality of the company that had been acquired. In Stefanini's case, many did not know its culture well and had questions about what would come ahead.

Graça Sajovic, Marco's wife, was next to him throughout the event, just as she had been present in Stefanini's history since the beginning, acting as vice-president. She was acutely aware of the cultural challenges that an integration like that could offer. She had already visited the branches and would continue to do so in the following years, which would give her a privileged perspective of how people from different countries behaved. This had started in Brazil. In the Northeast, they had a different schedule – work started earlier and ended earlier too. In Curitiba, she realized the employees were more reserved. Going further south, she noticed that people were more combative in their relationships. Each of these profiles had to be understood in order to avoid misunderstandings and achieve harmony.

The same thing happened in other countries. In many of them, for instance, employees have hierarchically-driven social relationships. In other words, they treat people very differently depending on the position they hold or even the social stratus they belong to, which on several occasions shocked a woman from São Paulo like Graça, used to hugging and talking to everyone. She once shared affectionate words with a cleaning worker at a foreign branch, who then burst into tears. According to the employee, no one had ever spoken to her like that, not there, not in any other company.

In the opposite direction, even Graça was startled to note that in Argentina all employees arrived in the morning and kissed each other. An employee would arrive and kiss everyone, including the country manager. Then another came, and yet another. All of them, every day.

When she started to interact with the new US branch, after the acquisition of TechTeam, she realized that her habit of blowing kisses and hugging was met with surprise. Other Brazilians quickly discovered the difference between cultures. An executive once decided to strike up a conversation at lunch.

"So, do you already know who you're going to vote for in the election?"

"We don't talk about politics," the other person answered, dryly, but with a slightly embarrassed smile, showing that they knew where the question was coming from. It was from another culture.

A much stronger reaction occurred when a Brazilian employee jokingly pinched an American employee's arm. This act may be understood as part of the playful Brazilian culture, but Americans greatly value their personal space. In this case, the employee ultimately resigned. Therefore, that which seems normal for one culture may be unacceptable for another.

Aware of this, Graça looked at the dinner table, with dozens of foreigners, and understood that the challenge was not restricted to management standards. Among the executives present at the event was the then business director, Marcelo Ciasca, who had moved to Mexico in 2004. He had firsthand experience of what cultural difference could entail for the success or failure of an international branch.

Born in São Paulo, Ciasca's youth had been far removed from technology. For five years, he pursued a career in the Army, leaving as an officer. This experience influenced how he saw people management. Not the forced discipline that people usually see in the military, but the ability to deal with individuals who often wished they were not there. He learned how to establish relationships in adverse situations and how to earn the respect of people with different profiles – different social classes and cultures.

From the Army, he went to work in computer sales and arrived at Stefanini in 2001. Three years later, he was invited to take over the business unit in Mexico, which at the time had barely half a dozen employees, allocated in an office of 50 m2. Ciasca accepted, thinking that if everything went well, he would stay two or three years. The reality was quite different than expected. And a valuable lesson for all Brazilians and foreigners at that dinner party.

This is because entering Mexico – as is the case in many countries – was quite difficult in the early years. Having started with Argentina in 1996, Chile and Mexico were the second movement in 2000. The following year, Stefanini arrived in Peru, Colombia and the United States, with the experience of Antonio Moreira finding the first American clients. Two years later, Spain, Portugal, and Italy. In 2006, it was time for the United Kingdom and India, and in 2008, Canada.

In each country, navigating the new culture had its challenges. In 2004, when Ciasca arrived in Mexico, the branch wasn't closing many deals yet and was losing money. Like Moreira in the United States, there was Ciasca, exploring the territory and communicating in a language that was not his own.

"¿Cómo estás?"

Ciasca's Spanish didn't go much further than asking how people were. Besides, he knew that learning to speak wasn't enough; being savvy enough to convince people was the key. He rushed to take Spanish lessons. He didn't have the luxury of getting anything wrong or making grammar errors in emails. To ensure greater integration, he decided to avoid the most often chosen path, which was to pick neighborhoods where many Brazilians live, such as Interlomas or Santa Fé. Those who did that ended up creating a Brazilian bubble around them, meeting neighbors on the weekend to have churrasco parties and speak Portuguese. Not Ciasca. He chose to live in Naucalpan, a town just over twenty kilometers from the capital, Mexico City. He also enrolled his children in a Mexican school, and the entire family immersed themselves in the local culture.

He gradually realized that the Mexican business culture was a little different from what he was used to in São Paulo. For instance, their relationship with time was different, with a verb tense Ciasca came to refer to as "ahorita." If they are asked to perform a task, they reply with:

– Ahorita yo hago.

In other words, "I'll do it in a little while." Which could mean in a minute or the day after. Coming from a military background, one would expect that Ciasca would try to eliminate this kind of reaction. This is the big mistake made by companies that seek to do business internationally: trying to impose their way of working on other cultures. Ciasca made no such mistake. While he knew the importance of discipline, he also understood how crucial it is to create good relationships in order to obtain good results. He responded to differences by creating deadlines while respecting the employees' autonomy to manage their own time. This was a perfect match with Stefanini's philosophy, which involves always giving everyone the freedom to define how to operate.

Over time, he realized that Mexicans heavily base their work relationships on personal relationships. This contrasts with more individualistic cultures, in which people isolate themselves in their separate rooms, do their work, and go home. Mexicans interact more, both with co-workers and with their partners. These connections make everyday life lighter, more creative, and full of possibilities.

By understanding this element, Ciasca was able to proceed with the Mexican operation, even though he could not count on acquisitions to take on the market. Unlike what happened in Uruguay and Colombia, where acquisitions allowed Stefanini to automatically gain customers, this never happened in Mexico. When the acquisition of TechTeam took place, bringing clients in several countries, especially in the United States and Europe, none were located in Mexico.

Ciasca moved forward organically while attempting to get used to a part of life in Mexico that terrified him: earthquakes. That was when the global financial market experienced its own seismic shock: the 2008-2009 crisis. At that time, he had already managed to establish the company as an alternative in the market, and the relationships built turned out to be useful. Thanks to this, Stefanini would, for the first time outside Brazil, live up to its reputation for growing in the midst of crises.

In the worst months of the economic turmoil, a representative from a major Mexican bank reached out and proposed:

– I'm going to pass on to you just over a hundred resources – referring to the employees of several companies providing technology services to the bank.

These service providers lacked the funds to pay the employees assigned to the bank. They also did not have enough credit to get money, since they were already leveraged by debt or other loans. At that moment, Stefanini had a great advantage, as it did not incur any debt. This would soon allow for the acquisition of TechTeam, as well as all acquisitions in the coming years. Stefanini's entire strategy would be enabled by the fact that it did not go into debt and had its own capital to fund its expansion.

This advantage also proved useful when the crisis hobbled Stefanini's competitors in Mexico. That's what made the bank executive contact Ciasca.

– You'll absorb these resources, and I'll enter a contract with you alone. – He paused and then concluded:

– And we'll then eliminate the other suppliers.

Ciasca started talking to potential customers, proposing that Stefanini could take over the services provided by competitors who did not have the financial capacity to support themselves. This also started to occur in other Latin American countries and in Brazil. Ultimately, as its competitors shrank, Stefanini grew in terms of revenue and size of operations.

When the crisis ended, and after the acquisition of TechTeam, Marco restructured the company at a global level, dividing it into four major regions: United States, Europe, Brazil, and Latin America (without Brazil, of course). In Mexico, the operation continued to grow. From a company without any notable presence, Stefanini became one of the 15 most important IT companies in the country.

As such, learning how to deal with a different culture and taking advantage of opportunities in crises, Ciasca ended up having to revise his plan of staying in Mexico for two or three years. He was assigned leadership over the Latin American region, becoming the CEO for Latin America. He continued to live in Mexico but began to travel around the region, alternating visits between Colombia, Peru, Chile, Argentina, and Uruguay. Instead of two years, his stay in Mexico would last almost 16 years, from 2004 until 2019.

Experiences like Ciasca's are difficult to convey, even more so in an event that would only last a few days like the 2011 kick-off. All those Brazilians and foreigners, whose diversity Graça admired so much, would return to their countries still wondering what the integration between Stefanini and their local culture would be like.

This included Belgian Tania Herrezeel, one of the executives responsible for TechTeam's operations in Europe. She experienced a situation that was almost the mirror opposite of Ciasca's. She had recently joined TechTeam and suddenly saw the business be acquired by a company from a country she knew very little about.

For Tania, the first contact with Marco had been stressful, as if she were at a job interview. After all, being a new employee, it was reasonable to assume that she would be replaced by a Brazilian executive. For the first time in her life, she faced the possibility of staying in a company for a short period. Despite being in the job market since the early 1990s, Tania had only worked at three companies. In the last one, before TechTeam, she stuck around for 17 years.

Brussels would be the second office Marco would visit after the acquisition, following his stint at TechTeam's Michigan headquarters. The Belgian capital was TechTeam's base on the European continent, which at the time had an operation the size of the US portfolio. Marco arrived in Brussels just before Christmas, greeted by a very blue sky and a sunny day, which seemed to add to the chilliness of that winter. He took the usual tour of the office, saying "good morning" to everyone, not unlike what he had done in Michigan. Finally, he called Tania over to talk. She walked into the room, wondering if this was the time she would say goodbye. Instead of a dismissal, Tania heard an invitation.

"We are organizing our customer database," Stefanini's founder explained.

Tania knew it was a strategic task, since they were aggregating information about new purchases with the TechTeam portfolio.

"You know all the agreements," he explained. "I want you to come to Brazil so we can understand how we are going to go about this."

So, in January 2011, Tania went to São Paulo, the first among all foreign executives to visit Stefanini's headquarters. She spent a week exchanging information with the Brazilians. The European client portfolio was very different from the Brazilian one, with most of the services related to the IT service desk. Most of them were global clients, always served in their local language, which means providing services in a dozen languages. Another major portion of services involved development, marketing, sales, and management.

This experience showed Tania how the way of working at Stefanini had some major differences in relation to what she was used to when dealing with Americans. Decisions were made quickly, and, although Marco was very present during the period she stayed in São Paulo, it was clear to her that the executives had great autonomy and made decisions without having to consult him all the time.

After integrating the customer database, Tania would return to Brazil to take part in the famous kick-off, with dozens of other foreign executives. She and others present at the event were already noticing Stefanini's autonomy-driven culture, which made some of them imagine that the company would probably replace the most important positions with Brazilians. After all, autonomy requires a certain amount of affinity, and it would be natural to think that an executive already used to the company would be more easily trusted. Perhaps, Tania thought, that historic dinner would be her first and last contact with Brazil and Stefanini.

But Marco decided not to make the same mistake as those companies that make preemptive strikes. He had no intention of "cleaning house" by eliminating local executives and imposing the Stefanini culture abruptly. Instead, he recognized the importance of preserving the local culture and the executives' relationships with the market. While he planned to eventually bring in Brazilians, his focus was on building a team primarily composed of local employees who would understand how Stefanini operated.

This approach allowed Marco to preserve the local culture, as well as maintain the executives' established relationships with the market. In Europe, for instance, no Brazilians were assigned, at least in the early years. Tania, like the others, remained at Stefanini. On that occasion, Marco successfully avoided a potential trap. However, he knew that other challenges would still arise in the future.

CHAPTER 14

IDENTITY

A fter the kick off, Tania returned to Brussels in order to finally deal with the everyday life at the new company. During her first video conference with Marco, a problem came up: she didn't quite understand what he was saying. On one side, a voice with a strong Brazilian accent and still lacking in fluency. On the European side, an extremely fluent English speaker, but not a native one. Tania started gesturing with one hand, miming what she was trying to say. With the other hand, she opened the Google Translate page and resorted to some words in Portuguese.

Besides the language barrier, another challenge emerged, one that was harder to overcome. Although the acquisition had brought clients and employees, it lacked a crucial element: a strong brand. "We're just another IT company," Tania contemplated about the operation before the acquisition. "We have good numbers, but nothing exceptional to offer." The company found itself in the European market as yet another American entity, without a history that could clearly define its identity. While having an American nationality associated with technology had its advantages, it was insufficient for differentiation.

This situation posed a challenge for Stefanini in presenting a completely new pitch. Tania embarked on a market tour to discuss the changes. Over the next few months, she reached out to existing clients and attended technology fairs in London and Barcelona.

During her conversations, Tania realized that Stefanini did have a story to tell.

"A Brazilian company, you say?" some would inquire, with a mix of skepticism and curiosity.

In the early years of Antonio Moreira's presence in the United States, he struggled to gain the attention of prospective clients. The company had no established relationships, its brand was unknown, and being a Brazilian company didn't help matters. However, Tania had already established relationships, and people were intrigued to learn about the Brazilians who had acquired an American company with existing European business.

"TechTeam was listed on Nasdaq, right?" they would ask. Typically, publicly traded companies with access to ample credit go on acquisition sprees, not the other way around.

Two years after the acquisition of TechTeam, in late 2012, Tania began to grasp the tangible sense that Stefanini had a genuine history. This realization came when the English version of the first edition of the book "The Child of Crisis" (then titled "The Son of the Crisis") was published. In her quest to understand what made this story distinctive, she delved into Marco's account of founding Stefanini and leading it to become a significant company in Brazil. The narrative culminated in the acquisition of TechTeam.

From that point onward, the book became a crucial tool in helping executives like Tania comprehend Stefanini's culture. In addition to profiling the founder, readers discovered how the company navigated major market transformations in the 1980s, 1990s, and 2000s. Outsourcing, downsizing, global crises— Stefanini possessed a history and a mindset ingrained in its culture. The company embraced reinvention when necessary, exhibited agility when required, and demonstrated intense flexibility, creativity, and resilience. Stefanini thrived even in crisis scenarios.

However, Stefanini was undergoing a complete transformation, and the story told in the book could not explain everything. Tania would have to figure out the rest through practical experience. Could Stefanini replicate its success in international operations? And if so, how would it work in such diverse cultures? In addition to the cultural challenge, Marco feared that the company's new size would make it slow, bureaucratic, and unwieldy. To him, agility was rooted in Stefanini's DNA, as well as his own personal ethos: being responsive, always available, and promptly engaging with customers. While larger corporations often felt the need for more planning, Marco was unsure if he wanted that need to hinder speed.

For the employees who now found themselves part of Stefanini, the answers to these questions, both in terms of culture and agility, were perceived through the rigidity or flexibility with which they received guidelines from the Brazilian headquarters. Until then, European employees were accustomed to being managed by an American company. Now, they were under a Brazilian company, whose business culture they knew very little about. Furthermore, it was a highly distinctive Brazilian company. An adaptation process was necessary.

Tania's doubts and discoveries were echoed in other Stefanini branches simultaneously—in Latin America, the United States, and Asia. What exactly was Stefanini's identity, and how could different cultures be integrated into it? The English version of the book reached all countries and aided in this process. At the end of 2013, the Spanish version was published. The book not only depicted the company's founding and growth story but also provided insights into why it was different from others. Nonetheless, it still didn't answer all the questions. The story continued after the acquisition.

The outcome depended greatly on the performance of those joining the company, as they were the new characters shaping the new Stefanini. One question was how they would respond to the company's culture. Would they stand up and abandon their Brazilian colleagues, as the Belgians once did with Ambev executives?

On one hand, it was crucial for Stefanini to respect the local culture of each country. However, it was also essential to have individuals who resonated with Stefanini's style. Vice President Graça Sajovic, who closely monitored the integration process, believed in considering certain personal attributes when selecting and hiring employees. Later, a group of professionals from different areas and countries summarized these characteristics as "seven attitudes." They were:

✓ Innovating with clients.
✓ Making a difference.
✓ Leading by example.
✓ Acting like an entrepreneur.
✓ Being ethical and consistent.
✓ Believing in people and respecting them.
✓ Being humble enough to learn.

According to Graça, most of these attitudes were related to a fundamental aspect of working at Stefanini: enjoying working with people. This was evident considering the company's strong focus on services. Quality service cannot be achieved without genuine care for people. The ongoing acquisitions could not fundamentally alter this trait.

In the process of cultural integration, this people-oriented focus became crucial. It was not only evident in the obvious aspects, such as ethics (item 5) or belief in people and respect for them (item 6), but also in the smallest details. Even three years after the acquisition, signs with the name of TechTeam could still be found in the American branch in Michigan, the former headquarters of the acquired company. Cultural integration was not an easy task, especially since Marco decided to proceed cautiously, fearing the mistakes made by other companies. Not all barriers had been dismantled, and employee proximity was still progressing slowly.

In the case of the American headquarters that Marco had visited, the decision was not to impose drastic changes. He believed in proceeding tactfully and not giving orders on how things should be done in the United States, as had happened in famous cases, such as the Chinese acquisition of a company in Ohio.

On the other hand, the European offices were accustomed to receiving guidance from the United States, so the transition was not as difficult. Moreover, Stefanini executives noticed that Europeans had a tendency to plan meticulously before taking action. This profile made them receptive to being assigned roles, meeting requirements, and adhering to rules.

However, Stefanini's culture was different. It was no longer just about following instructions. Instead, the company sought an entrepreneurial spirit. Autonomy and a sense of urgency gained importance. Terms like "entrepreneur," "mindset," and "ownership" became more significant in the company's jargon.

Every executive who joined Stefanini from different cultures and countries felt the difference. For example, Damian Mendez, an Argentinean who became the country manager in Argentina in 2014, had previously worked at Citibank for twenty years, familiarizing himself with the Latin American corporate market elite. Despite admiring the quality of processes he experienced with clients and partners, he perceived international companies as slow.

At Stefanini, Mendez discovered a different way of operating. Whenever a difficult decision had to be made, he would call Marco, and everything would be resolved within minutes. He noticed that Stefanini's founder adjusted his time according to the clients' needs. Conversations with Marco revolved less around strategy, profit, or technology, and focused more on specific clients. In contrast, when he spoke with Graça, the focus was on people. Mendez found this dichotomy between clients and people helped define Stefanini's focus clearly. He adapted well to this culture and eventually became the CEO of Stefanini Latin America in 2019, five years after joining the company.

Another executive who experienced a noticeable difference was Farlei Kothe, a Brazilian who joined the European branch in 2017. He would later become an important figure in Stefanini's history. Upon his arrival, Kothe noticed the high qualifications of the local professionals. They studied extensively, possessed excellent cultural knowledge, and spoke multiple languages fluently. They were thorough planners, and their results were consistently excellent. However, Kothe realized that changes were necessary.

It's not that he didn't value planning. On the contrary, his colleagues saw him as someone who was excessively focused on planning. But planning alone was not sufficient. Soon after establishing himself in Bucharest, the capital of Romania and Stefanini's main delivery base, a client requested a presentation with a two-day deadline.

When Kothe informed his team, he heard their skepticism: We'll have to decline, right?

What do you mean? - asked Kothe, a native of Rio Grande do Sul.

Well, it can't be done in two days. A presentation usually takes at least two or three weeks to prepare.

Kothe thought they were joking, as the time difference was too significant.

No, there's no way we can't do it - they insisted.

After the meeting, Kothe returned to his desk and started gathering material. He quickly put together a basic presentation and asked his team to help him review it the next day.

Eventually, they managed to complete the presentation by the requested deadline. The client was grateful that their request was handled within the expected time frame.

Kothe couldn't help but boast:

There you go, you thought it couldn't be done? It's done.

However, he said it calmly, knowing that this difference in perspective was a cultural issue and that the divergence was far from being resolved.

In fact, a few months later, Kothe realized that he wasn't effectively delivering information to clients in a timely manner. One of the methods they used was through workshops, but the process was slow because they typically organized individual workshops for each client. Kothe had an idea to improve efficiency and announced it to the team.

He proposed scheduling a workshop at their location instead of doing individual workshops for each client. The employees seemed to appreciate the idea, but there was a moment of surprise and concern when Kothe mentioned that he wanted to invite thirty clients and hold the workshop in-house. This meant that clients from various countries would need to attend, making the organization and logistics more challenging.

The team debated the details, such as the duration and essential topics of the workshop. Excitement began to build as everyone understood that it could work. However, one employee mentioned that it would take until the start of the third quarter to pace themselves and pull it off. Kothe was startled because it would mean waiting three months until the workshop took place, and any resulting projects wouldn't be implemented until November. He insisted they only had weeks to make it happen.

The room erupted with jeers, and some employees thought Kothe's idea was crazy and would be a disaster. They believed that sacrificing quality was not the right approach. However, Kothe saw it differently. He believed that taking a good action today would yield results, whereas waiting for an excellent action in the future would be a loss of opportunity.

Three weeks after the meeting, the workshop named "Digital Transformation Everywhere" took place. They managed to attract 70 participants from diverse industries such as banking, retail, and automotive, representing some of the world's largest companies. The clients loved it, and the team felt proud of their accomplishment.

Kothe realized that they had found a compromise, combining quality and timely execution. After the success of the first workshop, they adopted the same model for subsequent workshops in Spain, Belgium, and Germany, eventually turning it into a marketing tool for Stefanini.

Kothe's attitude aligned with what Graça described as "acting like an entrepreneur" and represented the corporate culture Stefanini wanted to foster. Employees were encouraged to decide the best course of action and utilize their knowledge and expertise to carry it out. However, this new way of working required an adaptation period, and some people embraced it while others chose to leave because it didn't align with their preferences.

In the first half of 2013, Marco visited Europe as part of his regular visits. Tania, a Belgian woman, noticed that Marco's fluency and command of the English language had improved since their initial long-distance contacts. Stefanini had provided executives with an application to help them learn Portuguese, and Tania was already falling in love with Brazil, its culture, and Stefanini's history.

Effective communication had always been crucial for Stefanini, especially during crises when Marco would directly address the entire company to explain their response to challenging situations. Marco considered communication with clients and employees to be one of his greatest strengths. However, as Ciasca had learned in Mexico, speaking a second language wasn't enough. Mastery had to be complete without any mistakes. It was essential to avoid misunderstandings where the client might say one thing, and Marco would understand something different, or vice versa.

The pilgrimage had begun, and Tania quickly noticed that Marco was a direct and pragmatic leader who cut through formalities and went straight to the heart of the matter. His questions were straightforward and focused on finding solutions to problems. This approach broke down the formal atmosphere that typically surrounded these meetings, and Marco spoke a universal language—the language of problem-solving. His behavior exemplified attitude 3, "leading by example."

After their first meeting, Tania realized that Marco was an approachable CEO unlike any she had experienced before. This might explain why he was always warmly welcomed, even when his command of the English language wasn't perfect. Whenever Tania asked, Marco willingly accompanied her to events and engaged with clients. He made an effort to meet with the CEOs of clients, even if they were from much larger companies than Stefanini. He would look them in the eye and say, in the best English he could muster, "I'll make sure my team here gives you the best."

Although it might sound like a marketing pitch, there was something genuinely different about Marco's approach—a warmth and openness that Brazilians, at least in their better moments, managed to show. In technical terms, Marco created what could be called a human-to-human approach, fostering personal connections with clients.

There was a similarity between this behavior and what Graça understood as the essence of the seven attitudes: "liking people." Over time, employees at each operation began to understand how Stefanini operated, and one of them was Kelly Gotha, the global sales director based in the United States. One day, the Chief Information Officer (CIO) of an important client, a major multinational company in the chemical industry, invited the Stefanini team to a charity auction.

During the auction, the prize was a special dinner prepared by a top chef, who would go to the house of the auction winner. The bidding became fierce, and it seemed like the CIO's table would secure the prize. But Kelly raised her hand, smiled, and proposed a bold move. She offered to cover the last bid if the CIO agreed to have the dinner take place at her house. This blurred the lines between personal and professional, as it was a culture that valued personal space. However, the CIO's contagious smile overcame any resistance, and the client accepted the proposal. The dinner took place with Graça, Marco, Kelly, and two other executives joining the client at her house to enjoy the chef-prepared meal.

These small but meaningful details defined Stefanini's identity. It wasn't just their ability to react to crises, but also the human and direct approach embodied by Marco and the Brazilians who joined the foreign branches. These were the attitudes that Graça valued when hiring, along with the autonomy given to employees.

In general, major corporations struggle to disseminate their values in places with significantly different cultures. While they can enforce procedures, creating a shared environment is much more challenging. Stefanini, however, managed to consolidate these characteristics and create the necessary conditions for the changes they knew were necessary.

The changes first became noticeable in the details. Three or four years after the acquisition, signs with the TechTeam name were no longer visible at the branches, and both employees and clients were already familiar with what it was like to work with this distinctively Brazilian company. When Graça sent an email to colleagues from cultures not typically associated with Brazil, their replies would be concluded with "kisses." The Brazilian joy seemed to infect everyone, and Stefanini's identity shone through.

However, the changes were still far from complete. It was not enough to be agile and ready for crises. Years later, Marco reflected that maybe he should have moved more quickly with the changes, not least because the global landscape in the IT sector was also changing rapidly. Being a resilient service company had become insufficient when it came to being considered competitive. Stefanini would need the commercial focus that had accompanied the company from the start; otherwise, it would stagnate and be swallowed up by the market.

CHAPTER 15

B U M P K I N S

"You don't know who I am, my name is Alex..."
Marco took a look at that young man who was
introducing himself during the 2012 CIAB
dinner. It took a split second, but he recognized
the lad. It was the young man who had given a lecture on
gamification. Marco didn't know, but Alex knew nothing about
it.

– I know who you are, you're the guy who gave that quirky
lecture on video games. Tell me more about what you do. The
Mato Grosso do Sul native, Alex Winetzki, spoke for three
minutes.

– That's interesting, I think I'm going to buy your company –
replied Stefanini's founder. Shortly after that surprising phrase,
the two said goodbye to each other. Winetzki immediately felt
that his life could change completely after that brief
conversation. All because he'd gotten up to introduce himself to
an executive in the middle of dinner and made a lightning-fast
pitch.

Going back home, Winetzki thought: "If he doesn't call me in
a week, I'll send him an email." Feeling the anxiety, he also
planned what he would do if the email went unanswered. "If he
doesn't reply in a week, it'll be because he had too much to drink
at that dinner party."

Born and graduated in economics in Mato Grosso do Sul, in
the capital Campo Grande, Winetzki decided he wanted to be an

entrepreneur and went to London in 2000. He spent seven years there working in tech startups. When he returned to Brazil, he no longer wanted to live in the land of soybeans and cattle, so he settled in Sorocaba, in the São Paulo countryside, where he had relatives. He made friends with an artificial intelligence professor at the Sorocaba School of Engineering, engineer Fábio Caversan.

In 2009, both set up a conventional software company, Woopi, which welcomed Caversan's top students. From Monday to Thursday, they made conventional software, dedicating Fridays to activities in what Winetzki pompously named the "Research and Development Center." It was Winetzki who described it as "pompously" because, in practice, this was a team of half a dozen colleagues who took a day to dream together. Deep down, the economist was trying to recover the joy he felt while innovating, which he had experienced in London. He paid the bills by making conventional software, but he sustained an ambition: to set up an artificial intelligence startup in Brazil.

That was when he had an exhilarating conversation with a friend about a new trend, the concept of gamification in the corporate market, and the other liked it so much that he extended an invitation for Winetzki to speak about the topic at CIAB. What this friend didn't know is that the economist didn't understand much more than what he had said during the conversation. Regardless, Winetzki said yes to the invitation, bought two books on Amazon, read them, and prepared a lecture. In the midst of a few dozen suits with very grave demeanor pointing at figures with a laser, Winetzki arrived with a humorous presentation full of light commentary. The organization liked it so much that they invited him to the dinner party, where he met Stefanini's founder.

Two days after his bold move at the CIAB dinner, a secretary called.

– Could you please come have a meeting with Marco Stefanini on Thursday at 8 am?

– Even if I couldn't before, I can now – Winetzki replied, a little nervously.

On the scheduled day and time, Winetzki and Caversan went to meet Marco. It was 2012, and most Brazilian IT entrepreneurs dreamed of setting up a startup to become millionaires after being acquired in large transactions by some multinational corporation.

After the pitch, Stefanini's founder said:

– Can I be frank?

– But I want to bring you into Stefanini.

And he made a modest offer to buy the small company with its staff of six. Winetzki and Caversan came back to Sorocaba a little disappointed to discover that their dream of instant riches was not going to happen.

They still said yes.

That's how, in October 2012, Woopi became Stefanini's ninth acquisition in three years. It was yet another part of an ongoing process at Stefanini: the quest to add value to the company's portfolio. After all, Marco was certain that expanding market access was not enough. A global brand can only stay in the game if it creates its own innovation ecosystem.

Each of the acquisitions had a very specific profile. The most important was still TechTeam, which almost doubled the company's size and consolidated the internationalization that had been taking place. But, even before TechTeam, other products arrived in the portfolio, with acquisitions such as the Brazilian companies Vanguard and Sunrising. Although these were small transactions, they brought strategic value, which began to be explored in the growing client portfolio.

In early 2011, shortly after the first kick off with dozens of foreigners arriving in São Paulo, the strategy continued with two more companies: the American CXI, a provider of technology services in the Virginia and Washington D.C. region, and the Colombian Informática & Tecnología, specialized in IT development. Marco was in a hurry and had cash on hand, so he was able to spend USD 100 million on both companies. And he warned the market that he still intended to invest another BRL 300 million in the following years.

Another year, another purchase, this time unlike all the previous ones: Orbitall. Rather than producing, implementing, or maintaining systems, the new acquisition handled credit and debit card processing for banks and retailers, including those of its owner, Itaú Unibanco. It was an important move for the seller, as Orbitall had already led the segment in Brazil before. However, it felt the need to reinvent itself; key customers had either left the company or were scheduled to leave.

For the buyer, Stefanini, this was an opportunity. It could transform the traditional processor into a provider of end-to-end payment solutions. And Orbitall was a "big fish," as they say in the market. Both for its net revenue, which in 2009 had been BRL 529.7 million, and for the number of employees it brought, more than two thousand people – all located in São Paulo – who now became part of Stefanini. This time, it would also be a different kind of absorption in cultural terms, as it brought a large contingent of employees who were not part of the sectors traditionally served by Stefanini. They thought and acted differently, at a different speed, and had a much greater expectation in terms of stability, almost like a government entity.

A few months later, another acquisition of a company with a very different culture: Uruguayan Top Systems. This time, it was a company that operated in the extremely traditional and closed-out segment of systems aimed at banks and finance companies. With that, Stefanini added a product to its portfolio for a very special and difficult-to-penetrate sector: software for "core banking," thus named because it was considered the heart of these companies, being responsible for processing transactions.

It was a month after the Top Systems acquisition was completed that Winetzki heard an unusual phrase during dinner at CIAB: "I think I'm going to buy your company." Marco was in a frantic pace. "I am planting the future," he would say.

There was something that united those two acquisitions, Woopi and Top Systems. Selling systems to banks was an extremely difficult gamble, as it was perhaps the most regulated and important type of software in the world, responsible for moving trillions in funds, whether in dollars, reais, or any other currency. In Woopi's case, the idea of "planting the future" was even more explicit, although no one – not even Marco – had any idea how this would take place.

This was how Winetzki and Caversan entered the narrative, with a bet on something that nobody knew before. They kept 49% of Woopi and sold the rest, becoming part of the Stefanini Group. At the time, the official narrative was that the small company from Sorocaba was specialized in "internet applications, portals, and software for the digital market." But, as Marco said in the heart-to-heart when they negotiated, Stefanini was already able to do everything they did. In October 2012, when the purchase was completed, three months after the first meeting at CIAB, the amount was not disclosed, as it was not relevant. The true investment would come later.

In fact, Marco's intention was to create a research and development hub. It was less about acquiring a company and more about attracting executives with the right profile to innovate. A selection that was able to recognize talents from a quick conversation. In spite of their initial disappointment, the "country bumpkins," as Winetzki used to say, saw an opportunity to do what they dreamed of: leaving the manufacture of conventional products behind and producing something that was truly avant-garde. "What do we do now?" thought Winetzki. The first step was to understand what Stefanini did.

At the time, executive Ailtom Nascimento, born in Rio de Janeiro and raised and educated in São Paulo, had returned to Stefanini after being on leave for two years. He came back as the vice president of global accounts, working on several fronts, but with an acute vision of trends in the corporate world and what Stefanini needed to do to remain competitive. He had noticed what he perceived as waves: the advancement of digitization in companies, first disseminating information internally, then externally, and finally reaching clients. He witnessed progress in terms of mobility, automation, and new technologies, which always promised to completely transform the corporate world and its relationship with customers. His challenge was to place Stefanini at the forefront of these movements and not be overwhelmed by them, as so many companies had been in the past.

Faced with all these trends and challenges, Woopi's members – Winetzki and Caversan – decided to focus on the customer service area, specifically the "service desk" sector. For the "country bumpkin" entrepreneurs, it would be ideal to try to unite the knowledge they had of artificial intelligence with the most common service within Stefanini.

"A virtual assistant could shorten the process," Winetzki suggested to the team in the first half of 2013.

He was initially met with skepticism, including from Woopi's own team.

"I don't believe this is going to work," one of the employees said, avoiding eye contact but summing up what everyone was thinking. They thought it was nonsense, that it made no sense.

From then on, Winetzki and Caversan began a long period of constantly convincing, both inside and outside Woopi. Most of the time, they had to behave like missionaries preaching a gospel.

In the first year, they didn't make much progress. Stefanini invested, the team researched, and Woopi operated at a loss. The fear also increased, as if they were enacting the fight of a very small David against a gigantic Goliath. In that first half of the 2010s, the only company in a position to invest and unite artificial intelligence and service was IBM, with its Watson platform. In simple terms, Woopi intended to take on Big Blue, as IBM was referred to, with a staff of half a dozen employees.

The team even tried to study Watson itself as an alternative, but the conclusion was that – for the intended purposes at that time – the software was too complex, expensive, and heavy to be deployed in customer service. Thus, Woopi's associates decided to move forward with the decision, one that was "somewhat stupid," as described by Winetzki, of building a platform from scratch.

With his head filled with doubt, the executive decided to call Marco.

"Marco, this isn't going to work," said Winetzki, explaining the current and future hardships of the project.

At the time, both he and Caversan were still unsure about the move they had made. They didn't feel like "executives at a multinational," but rather like they had joined a club for which they met no requirements.

"I think you might have bought the wrong guys," he suddenly said.

After a few seconds, he mustered the courage and asked:

– Perhaps we should go our separate ways?

In practice, this meant not only abandoning the artificial intelligence-driven service project but completely dismantling the company itself. The question indicated the level of frustration among Woopi's associates. Every executive reacts differently when faced with a situation of doubt, crisis, or nervousness. Depending on the situation, Marco would display different levels of enthusiasm. Often, his reply would portray a chilled-out tone, unlike what is expected from someone who is betting the future of their company and their own life. And it was with that surprisingly calm tone that he responded to Winetzki.

"Take it easy, my friend, it's going to work out."

Then came a word of encouragement, which showed that Marco understood that transitional moment for Winetzki.

"You'll soon get used to the speed of the game."

And he continued to invest in the company.

In the second year, the number of employees remained pretty much unchanged; now there were seven employees trying to accomplish the impossible. They hadn't hired any major names in artificial intelligence, especially because there was no one to hire in the first place. The sector's main development hubs were not located in Brazil, and the few Brazilians in the area were already comfortably established in larger corporations. All they had was a self-taught economist, Winetzki, a professor and doctoral student in artificial intelligence, Caversan, and his most talented students.

Marco once again insisted:

"It'll all work out. Let's not give up."

To this day, one can see that Winetzki, in addition to having strong admiration for Marco, does not quite understand why Stefanini's founder was so determined regarding that project.

Finally, a major leap forward in the project came when the team at Woopi decided to take a radically different path than most platforms used. At the time, IBM's Watson and the first competitors that appeared – almost always from corporations with many billions of dollars in revenue – used the so-called neural network technique. It was the most promising gamble for anyone who dreamed of one day developing a completely independent artificial intelligence. There was one major hurdle, however: the neural network required an enormous amount of data to work.

This requirement was incompatible with the needs of service desk clients. Winetzki concluded that they needed a chatbot that could work with less data. The solution was to take an entirely different approach, the semantic network, which could work with less data and was more specifically focused on human language. Faced with a market almost entirely taken over by the neural network, the decision of Woopi's associates could be another risky step by someone who had no true knowledge of the sector, going against what everyone would rather do.

The decision to insist, now on an unexplored path, was maintained. In the third year, they decided to hire some people, and the team grew slightly. It was around this time that a fundamental conversation took place. Carla Ferber, who at the time was Stefanini's US marketing manager, presented a complaint:

"Guys, this idea of a code providing the service..."

"What's the matter?"

"The problem is that no one understands any of this. How about we create a character to make this vision tangible?"

Over time, the character was given the name Sophie.

By then, Stefanini had stopped making large acquisitions. After purchasing Woopi, in the São Paulo countryside, at the end of 2012, Stefanini's board of executives decided to slow down. Interesting opportunities had become scarce, and the company was already present all over the world. The challenge became offering new products to current or future clients.

Meanwhile, the global race was heating up in the IT sector, especially in the biggest market of all, the US, where competition is fiercer. It is there that Asian, European, and Latin American competitors face each other and do their best to win the most coveted contracts in the world. Some are extremely commercially aggressive but fall short in the delivery. Others have quality but move slowly. Others still are small and struggle to be acknowledged as worthy competitors.

Major threats included the Indians, who nabbed a part of the applications market until they started winning infrastructure contracts. By then, Stefanini – which had carried out a successful integration after acquiring TechTeam – started to lose important clients. The same thing happened with giants in the sector. For instance, after a good performance in the years 2010 and 2011, the United States' IBM began to constantly dip in revenue.

In Stefanini's case, the company's culture allowed it to escape the crisis that afflicted the market. While the giants shrunk, the Brazilian multinational grew 11% in 2013, from BRL 1.9 billion to BRL 2.11 billion. The following year, even without acquisitions, it proved that the reason for its unique performance came down to its unique culture: it repeated the 11% mark, achieving the mark of BRL 2.35 billion in revenue. The following year, in 2015, it achieved 18% growth.

The shock came in 2016. Although Stefanini did not shrink like its larger competitors, it was unable to repeat the performance of previous years. The accelerated growth rate – a historic characteristic of Stefanini – had been lost. And not only in new operations; it also suffered in Brazil. Those most optimistic would rather point out that its performance was still above market levels and that the devaluation of the Brazilian currency was responsible for part of the loss. At the same time, some bets had proven to be more difficult to pay off. For instance, the expectation of advancing with digital transformation projects was dragging in some companies due to internal issues, such as political and cultural resistance.

Stefanini still managed to cut its losses by emphasizing agility; it lost major clients but managed to replace revenues by winning others over, including in the competitive American market. Still, the shock was there, which sounded an alarm; Stefanini could not afford to stop growing. It would have to react and do this on all fronts: with culture, being agile, offering innovation and advantages. And it did start reacting. The company invested in automation, eliminated "fat" where it could, and focused on its best part: its culture of flexibility, agility, and quality.

That was when Marco realized that he had taken too long to carry out the cultural transition in international operations. He managed to react, but not in the way he thought was possible. In retrospect, he concluded that the initial caution had paid off, but as the environment became more competitive, he realized that it had been overdone. "I should have acted sooner," he thought. It seemed that Stefanini's management energy had been depleted, that they had lost some of their entrepreneurial spirit. They needed to reactivate the initial concepts responsible for the company's success. It was time for a double shot of that entrepreneurial DNA that had worked well so many times before.

While Marco and the CEOs course-corrected their global cruise liner, in Sorocaba the Woopi team had grown, now boasting a few dozen people. At the same time, the gamble on the semantic network seemed to pay off, and Winetzki received word that major competitors had chosen to develop platforms that used neural and semantic networks simultaneously, which Woopi would also end up doing. The company had moved on from the haphazard design stage and now looked like a company with possibilities.

Two fundamental elements were still missing in Woopi's endeavor: lucrative clients and, consequently, profit. The first pilot took place in 2015, the same year they announced the name Sophie to the market. In the following year, they managed to put projects into operation for three clients. It was a relief to finally see the product being accepted by the market. Even so, the year ended at a loss.

The big turning point would come in the form of a selection process to serve the largest sports brand in the world, Nike. Stefanini had been placed in Gartner's famous "magic quadrant" as a leading service provider. This recognition assured the Brazilian company an invitation to present a proposal. When the opportunity came around, Gladis Orsi had just arrived from São Paulo in Michigan, the former headquarters of TechTeam and Stefanini's new base in the United States. Working in the company since 2005, she bumped into Marco in the hallways. She had just completed twelve years at the company, and the founder called her to talk, saying:

Gladis, tell me what you want. What do you expect from yourself in the company?

Noticing the employee's surprise, Marco asked her to reflect for a while, dividing her goals into short, medium, and long-term actions.

The next day, after hearing what she had planned, he replied:

We are going to do everything you established as a short-term action. Done.

Alright - she replied.

In the medium term, Gladis wanted to become an executive in São Paulo, so she told Marco that - to prepare herself - she wanted to take on a different region in Brazil first and then move back to São Paulo. In the long term, she dreamed of international experience.

Marco made a funny face, as if he was about to say something unpleasant.

Gladis, these ideas for the medium term are just more of the same, they won't do you justice.

Before she could get disappointed, he added:

You have to focus on the international experience first.

Coming from the São Paulo countryside - from the municipality of Tatuí, 55 kilometers away from the Woopi's offices in Sorocaba - Gladis imagined herself traveling to some Latin American country.

Marco quickly weighed the pros and cons of each region, according to what he understood to be her profile. In particular, he warned that in Latin America she would have to travel a lot throughout the year, visiting every country in the region. As a counter-argument, he had a suggestion.

One of our coolest regions is the United States...

Marco, you know that my English is not up to the task.

Oh, you'll manage - he replied, then explaining the true reason for choosing her for the position. - I need Stefanini DNA there, I need more people who have our culture to help create our global ecosystem.

At the time, the regional headquarters had been moved from Florida to Michigan, TechTeam's former headquarters. In the second half of 2015, after six months alternating between Brazil and the United States, Gladis settled permanently in the metropolitan area of Detroit, which in that year had reported temperatures of minus 25 degrees Celsius.

She arrived with the same challenges as so many other Brazilians in a foreign market, entrusted with facing a different culture without having mastered the English language first. And she would also have to deal with the added complication of being a young woman in a still predominantly male market. Even so, she took over as one of three commercial vice presidents in the region, being responsible for the American Midwest region, with states like Illinois, Missouri, Iowa, Michigan itself, where she was located, and the country of Canada. She answered to the new CEO of Stefanini North America and Asia Pacific, Spencer Gracias, and was soon looking for opportunities to put the Stefanini DNA into practice.

The possibility of serving Nike appeared as the ideal occasion to show what she and the entire Stefanini team could do. The scope of the project didn't frighten the team, as there were already several similar ones being executed, but the geographic scope and volume made it the major opportunity of the year. At the same time, they knew they were going to compete with the big guys because everyone wanted that account.

This is where the Stefanini culture made the difference because, even when competitors are extremely interested, the ability to respond appropriately can be expanded or limited according to the culture. Slow or agile, aggressive or cautious, each participant in the dispute would depend on their own DNA.

In Stefanini's case, the teams reacted with great enthusiasm since they realized that this was the chance everyone had been waiting for. All support areas - marketing, finance, legal, human resources, infrastructure - were mobilized. Each one of them saw their own role as essential, embodying the idea that each department, each cell, and each employee had autonomy to make decisions and do what was necessary to achieve the goal.

In addition to the DNA, other advantages were being produced within that same culture of innovation and daring. For instance, the Sophie platform. Every other company brought products that, on paper, promised to do the same thing. In the PowerPoint presentations, everyone stated that it would be possible to customize and integrate exactly like the customer wanted. However, even though this was promised in theory, almost all companies faced enormous difficulty when it came to making good on this promise.

Not Stefanini. Especially because the source code was company-owned, developed in-house, always with the aim of being lightweight and ready to be customized, increasing the freedom to do whatever the client asked. Meanwhile, competitors were using much heavier products. For each specific request, changes took longer and became more expensive. Either that or the supplier simply refused to do what the client, in this case Nike, was asking.

When Spencer and Gladis called Caversan and asked:

Can it be done?

Anything can be done; we just have to look at the cost and time - Woopi's associates replied.

With that, Gladis would reply to the client:

It can be done.

Meanwhile, other clients often heard the following from suppliers:

"This cannot be done."

Or worse:

"You are doing it wrong."

Which meant that not only could it not be done, but the client would be forced to change the internal process itself. For a long time, the market accepted impositions like these, understanding that it was a chance to absorb better practices. However, this idea, often positive, ended up transferring the burden of constantly adapting to the customer side. This was one of the ways in which Stefanini's flexibility became an important advantage. At the same time, the effort to serve the client required Stefanini to advance in terms of technology and global management, which forced Sophie to mature. In another culture, the client's need would likely be met with a negative response: "It's not possible." In Stefanini's case, flexibility made it work.

As the number of competing suppliers dwindled, Nike began visiting facilities that would be responsible for providing the service worldwide. The entire process took over a year. Finally, in 2017, the winner was announced. Stefanini had won the contract with the largest sports brand in the world and would be Nike's global provider of technical support services.

The Brazilian company had defeated global giants. Not only that: when the contract expired five years later, it was renewed. Definitive proof of the quality of its service and products, including Sophie. After Nike, other major contracts followed, mainly in the industry and service segments.

This turnaround was mostly due to Stefanini's second shot of culture. But it was also due to the offering of competitive products like Sophie. So much so that Caversan ended up moving to Michigan in 2018, taking over as director of research and development at Stefanini. Three years later, in 2021, he was named vice president of digital innovation and innovation. In

Gladis' words, Woopi's platform had become a product that "annoyed" the competition, the advantage in each contract, the "cherry on top."

Sophie's success, with the product becoming fully mature in 2018, finally brought a profit to Woopi, with more than 60% of the revenue coming from outside Brazil, with four customers in Europe and 33 in the North America and Asia Pacific region, where more than 90% of the portfolio already used the platform. In Brazil, 64 companies were already using it. The projects started in the IT area's service desk, but other client areas, such as human resources or customer service, became interested and ended up implementing the platform. This was the Hail Mary shot for the Sorocaba team, which proved that their apparently unfeasible project was possible.

The Stefanini group managed to become the first company in the USD 1 billion revenue range to develop customer service driven by artificial intelligence. Currently, Woopi's team, which started with half a dozen employees, already has a staff of over one hundred people, including mathematicians, engineers, and linguists, bringing together a profile completely unlike that of the rest of Stefanini. Part of the team is located in Michigan, along with Caversan. His students, who joined at the very beginning, aged 18 or 19, are now just over 30 years old. Despite their youth, they are among the most respected professionals in the market in the elite area of artificial intelligence. In 2022, Woopi partnered with Microsoft to offer a universal machine translation application, initially working with 16 languages. The user speaks, and the software translates it in real-time for an audience, whether at a meeting or a lecture.

Meanwhile, the American operation continued to grow. It would still face a great challenge, in one of the greatest global crises of our time. But, before that happened, the Stefanini

Group's attention would turn to an acquisition that had faced a difficult first few years, that of Top Systems, in the apparently inaccessible core banking segment.

CHAPTER 16

HEART

“For those who wish to stay, I promise that the situation will improve.”

These were the words of Jorge Iglesias from Rio Grande do Sul. Before him, an audience of a few dozen Uruguayans, all of whom were employed at Top Systems, a software developer for companies in the financial sector that Stefanini had acquired four years earlier. The mood was hostile.

There were good reasons for them not to believe in Iglesias' promise in July 2016. When Top Systems was acquired in 2012, some of the associates remained on board. A deal was struck with them: changes would be made in management, aiming at growth. However, each of the parties understood that concept differently. Top Systems was a company positioned in an industry with no tradition of hard selling, with long-term clients who valued stability over innovation. It was a reasonable approach, considering that this is what banks had been looking for up until then. However, the world was changing.

By betting on the software segment for financial institutions, Marco and the other Stefanini executives knew that a change would come. For that investment to work, it would be necessary to go after new clients. Until the acquisition in 2012, Top Systems had a solid and faithful portfolio of 30 companies that used its products. But market transformations were not kind to those who bet on the past. Upon his arrival in July, Iglesias discovered that in the previous month, Top Systems had already rescheduled its employees' salaries. It was likely to happen again. The audience before him didn't have much hope that he could do anything about it.

Outside Top Systems, no one understood how the company could have gotten into this situation. Its product was Topaz, meant for the heart of financial systems, which is why this type of software is called "core banking." Launched in 1988, it was always intended to be taken to other countries. Two years later, they already set foot outside Uruguay, entering Colombia, Panama, and the United States. In the following years, they spread to eight more countries. At the end of the decade, they entered the European market.

The 2000s saw the company slow down a bit, but everything indicated that the desire to take on the world remained. When it was acquired by Stefanini, two other countries – Honduras and Nicaragua – became part of the client portfolio. In total, Top Systems had already managed to bring the toughest-selling product in the IT industry to 15 countries. Observing this trajectory, Marco made the purchase and established a goal: to be the largest technology company specializing in digital financial solutions, adding more products to the financial market, and continuing to expand to other regions.

However, four years later, the scenario was that of a stagnant company. After Nicaragua, Top Systems had not entered any other country. Worse than that, there were cash flow problems, and wages were being delayed. In the beginning, the situation could even be compared with that of Woopi, which operated in a segment that was new for Stefanini, and in which the transfer of culture was more difficult than when they acquired service companies. In that case, however, Caversan and Winetzki were imbued with the desire to grow. At Top Systems, the will to expand seemed to have disappeared.

This was the situation Iglesias was tasked with changing. Born in Porto Alegre, he had the energy of a young man, about to turn 40. He had spent his entire career focused on technology and management in the banking segment. Working on a joint venture between Getnet and Santander, he witnessed the transition from a fragmented market – in which each establishment was required to have several card machines, one for each brand – to a scenario in which a single machine accepted all brands. This market disruption experience showed Iglesias that it was possible to change the status quo. He learned that radical change, even when unlikely, was possible.

Iglesias joined Stefanini to work on a strategic SAP Banking integration project and stayed. That is until Marco called him to talk about Top Systems. He reported that he had increased Stefanini's stake and now held 80% of the company. And he extended an invitation for him to direct it.

The Rio Grande do Sul native was fascinated. He already knew about the company and believed there was much to be done there.

– It's a precious gem, waiting to be polished.

A short while later, Iglesias disembarked with his entire family in Montevideo. And no one else. He took no staff, not even a single employee. He alone would face the Topaz team.

After the presentation to the employees, Iglesias went after the clients. The company's Ebitda was negative, that is, after paying interest, taxes, and discounting asset depreciation and loan amortization, there was simply no money. Top Systems was operating at a loss. Iglesias urgently needed to change that if he was to keep his promise that things were going to get better. Especially because he had made a commitment with those who decided to stay.

The first order of business was to regularize the cash flow. He spent the next few months calling clients and asking them to advance payments. At the same time, he needed to make a profound transformation happen.

In a meeting in the first year, he heard things that would discourage anyone.

– I don't want to serve this client – said an employee.

– It's going to be too much work – another predicted.

Often, because it was about prospecting for a project in a country that had not yet been served, other times because the client's environment was very different from the one in which they worked. That is, common situations that do not usually frighten professionals looking for new territories. Words like those made it clear that a part of the team was only comfortable with the portfolio they already had. Iglesias had to truly start "preaching" in order to imbue the team with the necessary energy and bring Stefanini's culture and drive to them. "We are starting a new company", he said.

All that pressure took a toll on Iglesias. The stress made him put on weight, and for a while he even got sick. He was constantly backed by Marco and Graça, who were always a phone call away, but that was all. Without bringing anyone with him from Brazil, he was left with the responsibility of transforming the team's culture. He needed to indoctrinate, establish a relationship of trust, identify the right people and – while doing so – keep the company on its feet. More so than the language barrier, as Ciasca had faced in Mexico, Iglesias noticed that there was a certain formality in the way Uruguayans communicated, quite different from the Brazilian informal style.

Meanwhile, Iglesias figured out what was set for and against him in the endeavor. Similar to what Stefanini executives found in Europe, Uruguayans also felt more comfortable with a more structured action plan. They needed to master the variables they were facing and to have enough time to do so. It was necessary to reconcile this profile with the sense of urgency, required both for their difficult situation and for Stefanini's culture.

On the other hand, there were excellent professionals available. Despite being a small country, with just under 3.5 million inhabitants, Uruguay always ranks highly when it comes to the best education in Latin America. It was the first country in the region to establish universal and free primary education in the 19th century. Brazil would only do so over a hundred years later. Public schools are known for their high quality and were digitized in the late 2000s. When he thought about the hardships, Iglesias forced himself to remember the enormous advantages of being in Uruguay. Many companies are looking for locations with abundant labor, but he knew that this was the best country in the Americas when it came to quality.

It was with this highly qualified workforce, yet comfortable with what it had achieved, that Iglesias needed to interact in order to enact the necessary changes. This included the product, which, with its three decades, was consolidated, but needed to be updated. Both main product meant for core banking and product for anti-money laundering measures.

One of the causes of the change was that, until that moment, replacing a core banking application was a prohibitive process for a financial institution. The cost was so high and the risk so significant that most large banks were forever "married" to their suppliers. Either that or they chose to keep development in-house, with all the costs and competitive disadvantages that this entailed. Several changes in technology and in customer behavior have caused companies to change their stance, starting to look for new and more modern technological solutions.

Knowing all this, Iglesias needed to prepare, perfecting the product and adjusting the team's culture to respond more quickly to the clients' needs. When it came to the former, he needed the product to be transactional, efficient and scalable. And it wasn't just a technological approach. For the executive, it was also necessary to redirect the focus. Before, the only concern was doing what the client wanted, which in theory aligned with Stefanini's culture. But the transformations in the market indicated to Iglesias that it was even more important to think about what the end user, such as the bank account holder, needed. Just as Topaz was at the heart of banking systems, Iglesias began to place the user at the center, at the heart of Topaz itself.

In short, the challenge was to transform two individual products into something different: a platform ready to be integrated into a larger set of solutions, focused on digital transformation with "the desire to work together to produce extraordinary results for customers", in the words of Iglesias. This is what would then be called a Full Banking Platform. When it became ready, the plan was to drop the Top Systems name, replacing it with the product name: Topaz. And instead of one or two systems or modules, an entire ecosystem, a "platform specialized in digital solutions for financial institutions." This would take time; the goal would still require some years to be achieved.

The following year, in 2017, the initial wave of modernization had been carried out, which helped with the first major achievement: entering Argentina. After thirty years of existence, the Topaz product finally arrived in the neighboring country to the west. A few months later, another crucial sale: the first product sold to a Brazilian company, Uruguay's neighbor to the north. It boggles the mind that it took three decades for the

Uruguayan product to reach its next-door neighbors, the two largest markets in South America. In just over a year, the team managed to customize the product for both countries, redirect the offer towards the platform concept and conquer new territories.

– We truly have the "crown jewel" here – Iglesias said to Marco in one of their telephone conversations, celebrating their entry into the two new markets.

However, the celebration included an awareness that those initial victories were only the first stage of a plan that was still in progress. And that broader vision encompassed both product and geographic expansion.

For this goal to be achieved, Stefanini would have to go shopping again. Or, to be more precise, Topaz – having put its cash in order after the 2016 crisis – would have to search for acquisitions. Iglesias intended to make the investments with the company's own cash, without loans or even asking Stefanini for help. Therefore, while the Topaz platform underwent modifications, he and the team scoured the market in search of mature and quality technological solutions, in the clients' perception. They wanted companies that had in-house intellectual capital and that had proven as much externally, with their product being used in Latin America, with the potential for it to be "scaled up." That is, that they could take that offer to other countries and customers.

The Topaz platform was finally announced to the market in 2019. The international scaling up was accelerated. In the following years, they would win over a total of ten core banking customers in Brazil alone, not to mention the rest of Latin America. In a market where this type of sale was extremely rare, the numbers and speed were jaw-dropping. A new power was rising.

At the same time, after two years of relentless pursuit, the first targets for acquisitions were identified in early 2020. These were two business units of the century-old American company Diebold Nixdorf. One of them was the OFD (Online Fraud Detection), created to protect digital channels and transactions. With 18 years of existence, it had been used by 40 clients, including banks, brokers, and companies in the financial sector, protecting over 200 million transactions per month with 70 million end users. Merely two years later, that number would reach 120 million users.

The other unit acquired from the American company was Servcore, with solutions used by 30 companies, such as employee integration (or onboarding), digital channels, and customer service automation. For almost a year, the two companies negotiated, and at that stage Marco increased his involvement, working out the details of the transaction. There were hurdles in this interaction, with a three-decade-old Brazilian company seeking to remove two strategic units from a 160-year-old corporation; both with billionaire revenues and presence in dozens of countries. Here, not only the source codes were crucial, but also the combination of those products with the 200 employees of the units, who jointly represented an intellectual capital of enormous strategic importance. Finally, in early December 2020, when Marco was celebrating his 60th birthday, the news reached the market.

That year had been unparalleled, both for the world and for Stefanini. The pandemic forced every person on the planet to live and work in a different way. In spite of these events, the acquisitions did not stop. The opposite was true, and the Diebold case was just one example. In the same year, Iglesias would also see BankPro from Rio de Janeiro join Topaz's portfolio to control and manage operations in the Open Market. In this case,

Stefanini already had a stake, and Marco acquired what was left, thus owning 100% of the company.

It wasn't just Iglesias who witnessed the arrival of new products and employees. The entire Stefanini Group had resumed purchasing intensely in recent years. That same month, Marco had concluded the acquisition of the consulting firms N1 IT, in the IT sector, and Senior Engenharia, in the electrical engineering and industrial automation area. Before that, also in 2020, Stefanini had acquired Logbank, which dealt with digital payments, the startup Mozaiko, specialized in data analysis for retail, and the digital marketing group Haus. With all this aggressiveness, the group now encompassed 20 companies operating in 41 countries.

Part of these acquisitions took place in the area of digital solutions and were grouped under a group accelerator, which was named Stefanini Ventures. Started at the same time as the entirety of Top Systems was acquired and Iglesias arrived in Montevideo, in 2016, the Stefanini Ventures team received, in the following years, between 30 and 40 proposals to be analyzed per month. Almost all of them were rejected. Those that managed to surpass the extremely strict screening showed their results in numbers. From the creation of the group until 2021, the acquired companies' revenue has increased six-fold, and their Ebitda has been multiplied by 15. Those responsible for the performance included, in addition to Jorge at Topaz, young Guilherme Stefanini, Marco's eldest son.

Among the new acquisitions at the end of 2020, the Haus group would have a special impact for Stefanini and a specific importance for Guilherme. After proving his ability at Ventures, the executive was given the mission to strengthen the group's digital marketing ecosystem, which Marco believed to have enormous growth potential for the coming years. That's how

Guilherme took over Gauge, a consultancy for digital products, such as Inspiring (engagement platform), HUIA (digital commerce), Brooke (digital content producer), among others that arrived. When the Haus group was acquired at the end of 2020, Guilherme placed all of them under this umbrella, integrating all offers within a single platform.

Likewise, the success of Ventures boosted a new project for the future: the area of capturing and accelerating opportunities would leave the "mothership" Stefanini and become a venture capital fund with BRL 300 million to invest in startups and new companies.

The cases of Haus and Topaz demonstrated a significant shift in Stefanini's structure. It transformed from a major corporation with a singular focus into a diverse group with divisions capable of exploring various market trends simultaneously. Winetzki's efforts with Woopi, creating a team with a distinct profile from the rest of Stefanini, took on a new meaning. Instead of one unified Stefanini, there were now multiple entities united by the DNA of flexibility, agility, autonomy, entrepreneurship, and the potential for synergies.

Topaz, in particular, evolved into a self-sustaining company by expanding its financial solutions. It gained autonomy in terms of financial resources, time, and strategic objectives, allowing it to consider acquisitions independently. It ceased being merely a business unit and became a company capable of conducting its own IPO and potentially entering the market before Stefanini itself.

To achieve this goal, Iglesias needed to complete the platform. In 2021, Marco faced tough competition from a multinational corporation during a lengthy negotiation to acquire a company. Initially, it seemed like a losing battle, but the target company realized that the multinational only intended to use it as a gateway to enter the Brazilian market. This revealed the multinational's lack of concern for long-term strategic objectives. Making such a mistake is a common pitfall in the market, as buying a business is relatively easy, but acquiring it with a strategic vision is challenging. Purchasing without considering long-term goals often leads to the waste of intellectual capital, the departure of partners and talent, and the decline of the acquired product. Numerous major corporations have lost billions of dollars due to such missteps.

The disputed company, CRK, specialized in integrated systems for financial management, particularly bank treasuries and instant payments. It was a pioneer in integrating with the Brazilian Payment System (SPB). Marco utilized his experience gained from TechTeam's operations to negotiate with CRK's four partners, ensuring the preservation of the company's structure, retention of talented professionals, and substantial investments in its products. This approach allowed Marco and his team to win the dispute against the competing multinational.

Following the acquisition, Topaz's workforce grew to 650 employees, serving 190 clients. Gartner, a leading IT market consultancy, recognized Topaz as the most comprehensive and compliant core banking technology platform for Latin America. However, the significant leap occurred in 2022 when Topaz acquired Cobiscorp, a company with a history slightly longer than Topaz's own existence, operating for nearly 70 years. Cobiscorp, founded in Ecuador and headquartered in the United States, served over 70 banks across Latin America's major countries. This transaction marked the first time Stefanini contributed to a Topaz acquisition financially. It became the second-largest investment in the history of the Stefanini Group since TechTeam. In a way, Cobiscorp paralleled TechTeam's significance for Topaz. Within a month, Topaz's employee count reached 1,300, serving 250 customers across 25 countries. Notably, this growth was remarkable when compared to the 70 employees and 30 customers present when Iglesias first arrived in Montevideo in 2016.

With the acquisition of Cobiscorp, Topaz became the sole company on the continent to offer core banking services in both Hispanic Latin America and Brazil. Its competitors were limited to either Brazil or the rest of Latin America. Additionally, according to Gartner, Topaz became the only market player with two banking cores, one of which was third-generation and entirely cloud-native.

These acquisitions posed a significant challenge for Iglesias. Cultural integration needed to be skillfully managed, as it was not just about buying companies from the market. In addition to instilling the Stefanini DNA into the newly acquired teams, Iglesias had to integrate highly complex products that needed to function seamlessly within the demanding corporate environment of the banking sector. Within the past two years alone, four companies had been integrated. Iglesias had the daunting task of bringing them all together without dropping the ball, missing opportunities, and ensuring everyone aligned with the same objectives. People who encountered Iglesias, who was 46 years old in 2022, often commented that he seemed overwhelmed by the responsibilities.

However, there were significant advantages as well. By selling a product within a platform, Topaz doubled its value proposition. Customers who hastily purchase individual applications from separate suppliers to meet their immediate needs often face future risks. They end up spending additional money to integrate these applications or even discarding them and buying from another supplier altogether. At Topaz, Iglesias could now offer a fully integrated solution that was prepared for future modules. This comprehensive offering arrived at the right time, as the market shifted away from buying individual functionalities and favored all-encompassing platforms that catered to end-to-end needs.

Topaz was well-prepared for the evolving market dynamics. Major banks aimed to transition into digital banks, while fintechs sought to become full-fledged banks. Powerful newcomers, such as retailers and telecommunication operators, also entered the scene from abroad, competing for customers who were open to receiving financial services outside traditional banks. Gartner predicted that a portion of consumers would choose to save time and reduce their interactions with conventional banks. For instance, customers could access their bank accounts through transportation apps, payment services, or e-commerce platforms to check their balances or credit facilities.

These changing market dynamics, coupled with the potential to serve tens of millions of unbanked individuals in Latin America, presented new opportunities for financial systems, and Topaz emerged as the best-positioned party to cater to these companies. In 2021, Topaz concluded a project with one of the largest retail chains in Brazil, bringing financial services into its stores. Within just three months, the client set a market record by opening over 1 million checking accounts. Meanwhile, Topaz was already working on a similar project with another global retail giant. Similar achievements were observed in other sectors such as telecommunications, media, fintechs, and credit unions, in addition to traditional banks. A prominent Brazilian bank, known for its rigorous technology assessments, evaluated Topaz's banking core for three years before finally selecting it for use in its digital arm in 2022.

An established credit union, recognizing that its customer base was aging and that younger customers were disengaging or uninterested, revamped its positioning, digitized its services, and implemented Topaz's banking core. By 2022, the credit union had already attracted over 5 million customers.

The scale of transactions and customer numbers was impressive. With just one relatively new Brazilian company in the payments sector, the Topaz platform processed ten million transactions daily. Since implementing the product, the customer multiplied its volume ten-fold, growing from two million customers to twenty million consumers of financial services.

Despite the economic crisis caused by the pandemic and the international geopolitical situation, Topaz continued to achieve its average annual organic growth of 30% to 40% over the past three years, in addition to growth through acquisitions. In 2022, it was projected to surpass annual revenues of BRL 600 million. Except for Central America, where a few countries were yet to be covered, Topaz had a presence throughout the entire American continent.

As Topaz made strides in the market, Iglesias pondered the trends that would shape the coming years. Possibilities included cryptocurrency, blockchain, artificial intelligence, open finance, cybersecurity, new digital channels, or other significant changes. However, regardless of the distant future, Iglesias and Stefanini executives were certain that the world was undergoing profound transformations, many of which were accelerated by the pandemic, reshaping the way the Stefanini Group operated.

CHAPTER 17

PANDEMIC

The conversation was repeated multiple times during Stefanini's global kickoff in January 2020. Farlei Kothe, CEO of Stefanini in the Europe, Middle East, and Africa regions, expressed his belief that remote work had become a new trend.

However, his interlocutors, including Marco Stefanini himself, remained skeptical and insisted that clients would not accept remote work as a viable option. Despite Kothe's assertions, the skeptics remained unconvinced about the feasibility of implementing remote work in the context of their client relationships.

The idea was not new; a few years prior, the issue had been discussed among executives who were aware of the many advantages of remote work. By working from home, employees did not need to travel and had an improved quality of life. It was also beneficial for Stefanini, as it allowed for expanded hiring options. If the commute to the office was eliminated, job positions would become interesting for many more people, and Stefanini would no longer be restricted to large urban concentrations, being able to hire people from virtually anywhere in the world. Talent would come first, instead of the neighborhood or city where the professional lived.

Despite the advantages, in practice, the idea still faced resistance in the market, both inside and outside Stefanini. There were still questions about whether employees would have the discipline to work from home and whether productivity would remain constant. Distractions could range from minding small children to unclogging sinks, not to mention infrastructure issues. In Kothe's case, European culture brought other kinds of challenges. Europeans were disciplined, yes, but their customers were also conservative, with a preference for face-to-face, planned, and timely service. As the executives would say, working hours should "start at 8 am, not 8:01 am."

Therefore, instead of sending people to work remotely, the Rio Grande do Sul native Kothe had just received instructions to rent another floor in the office he occupied in Romania. The executive had his reasons for resisting. In Europe, infrastructure and rent costs were very high, some of the most expensive among Stefanini's operating regions. And he had what they call a "good problem." Business was growing, and there was a need to expand, but there was no more room in the offices. Expanding or renting new premises was prohibitive, considering the costs involved. The operation would certainly become less profitable.

Kothe came back to Romania, wondering how to resolve the dilemma. He had arrived in the country three years prior, in early 2017, when the country's membership in the European Union completed ten years. Upon landing in the capital, Bucharest, for the first time, he was delighted with the city of just under two million inhabitants. When exploring the Romanian south, near the famous Danube River, he was reminded of his hometown, Santa Cruz do Sul. When visiting the Romanian Carpathian Mountains, he felt as if he were strolling through the towns of Gramado or Canela.

Romania had been chosen by Stefanini for its unique characteristics within the continent: a country with lower costs but with an impressive workforce, well-educated and able to speak many languages, residing in a geopolitically stable country. Unlike its neighboring countries, like the Slavic countries or Magyar Hungary, Romania is a Latin enclave. Its inhabitants find it easy to learn Spanish, Italian, and French – so it is common to find people who speak these languages, in addition to English and German. Like Stefanini becoming a multicultural company, Romania was a geographical and cultural crossroads, rich in its incredible diversity. It was the ideal place for Stefanini to establish its delivery center for the region.

Since arriving in Bucharest in 2017, Kothe has been known for never giving up on the ideas he believes in. Like when he wanted to put together a presentation in two days, in an environment that preferred to methodically study the client and deliver the presentation in three weeks. Or when he decided to invite dozens of clients to a workshop, giving the team three weeks to organize it. Kothe insisted on trading the best for the good because the latter brought results, and, little by little, he showed the European team that his way of thinking could work.

His fighting style worked because he was easy to talk to, but also because at the same time he was extremely rational, the typical tech nerd. Partly because he had spent his entire career in IT. From an internship as a programmer, through systems analysis, architecture, and business, to project management. At some point, he made the decision to change his career, in the famous "Y career" movement, deciding to migrate to the business area. The "nerd" took an MBA and ended up at Stefanini. He took care of the software factory in Rio Grande do Sul, going through Paraná, Brasília, and Rio de Janeiro before taking on the vice-presidency in Bucharest. Although he had spent many years on the sales team, as he says, he didn't have the background of a salesperson.

After returning from the kick-off in Brazil, in February, he organized his own regional kick-off. He took the entire Stefanini management team allocated in Europe, the Middle East, and Africa (a bloc known by the acronym EMEA) to a three-day event in Bucharest. At the time, 5% of employees were working remotely, a higher average than the rest of the company.

In front of the 130 employees present, the Rio Grande do Sul native declared his goal:

– I want 20% of European teams working from home – he said, bracing for the reaction. Some had their jaws drop to the floor, while others' eyes widened.

To say there was resistance is putting it lightly. Employees were almost as skeptical of Kothe's plan as the Brazilian board was in São Paulo. At that time, among the thousands of employees in Europe, the 5% working from home represented just 150 people. The subject of the pandemic was present, but the countries where Stefanini had the most staff – Romania, Poland, and Moldova – had not yet been greatly affected.

"Kothe, many clients won't accept it," summarized a man in the front row, voicing everyone's thoughts. It was that simple. The opinions or desires of each person didn't matter much. If the clients made a steadfast objection, Kothe's plan would be dead in the water.

With a structure different from the one in Brazil, the European operation largely served the IT needs of clients, in the so-called "service desk." These clients were global corporations, often with several different languages within the same company. But Stefanini always provided assistance in the client's language, even when in Poland, Romania, or Moldova. Another portion of the services involved development, marketing, sales, and management. These were the clients who would need to be convinced to be served by employees working from home.

At the same time that this debate was taking place at Stefanini, there was news of a new virus: the severe acute respiratory syndrome coronavirus 2, SARS-CoV-2. It caused a disease that was named COVID-19. The first infection was recorded near the Chinese city of Wuhan in November 2019, and the first death occurred in January. However, in the Americas and even in Europe, the virus was not yet seen as a global threat. The topic had been discussed at the January kick-off in Brazil and was the subject of debate, but not as something that could have a significant impact on the business.

However, that situation was about to change. While Kothe carried out the kick-off in the first half of February, COVID-19 had already caused hundreds of deaths in Asia, with record levels of infection worldwide. In this context, the most skeptical in Stefanini Europe eventually agreed that Kothe's idea came at the right time. In Brussels, Tania was also beginning to worry. Although there was only one confirmed case in the country, of a Belgian returning from Wuhan – there were no cases of domestic transmission – the executive watched the news on the continent carefully, especially regarding Italy, the first country to suspend flights from China. But she knew that few people in the business world – especially in Brazil – believed that this virus would have the power to paralyze the world.

Meanwhile, Kothe moved forward with his plan, which was considered bold. After the kick-off in Bucharest, the rotation began, with 20% of employees working from home. Every other day, he sent a small group home. In each rotation, he made adjustments to the infrastructure and paid attention to the level of service with customers. By the end of February, the tragedy that would shake Italy began to be translated into numbers, with several deaths recorded in the country and several cities in the north entering lockdown. Kothe had no more doubt in his mind. "We're going to have to speed this up."

Teams began to map which contracts and teams could be migrated to the remote approach without impacting contracts or being subject to fines. They also began to assess possible risks to enable secure remote access to systems.

At the end of the month, Farlei had already managed to send around 30% of his employees home. Just in time, because by then all of Europe began to panic. That's because the news coming from Italy got even worse in the first half of March. There were tens of thousands of cases, with deaths already surpassing the thousands. In the following days, hundreds of Italians would die each day from the virus. However, political and business leaders in Brazil – and throughout the American continent – did not yet believe that the region would be affected in the same way. So Kothe made his moves in Romania without much of a fuss.

In Brazil, executives assessed the global situation and concluded that it was manageable. The Italian catastrophe felt overwhelming, but Stefanini did not have large teams in the country. The delivery centers that served clients, including Italians, were located in Romania, Moldova, and Poland.

Tania felt differently. She feared for her life. From the Belgian's point of view, Italy was right at her doorstep, like someone from Rio de Janeiro thinks about São Paulo. When talking to executives outside Europe, she did not make the extent of her fear explicit but always asked about the possibility of engaging in remote work. The answer was always the same: it's just some kind of flu. Those who spoke of lockdown were certainly exaggerating. Concerned, Tania alerted Marco and Graça via WhatsApp, warning them that COVID-19 was much more serious than the flu.

The alert was understood, but at that time, nobody believed that what was happening in Europe and Asia could be repeated in Latin American countries. Among the executives who sought to assess the problem was Marcelo Ciasca, who had returned to Brazil in 2019, where he was in charge of the Latin American operation. In that first week of March, he checked the numbers again and confirmed that no deaths had been reported in the entire region. Nine countries confirmed cases, but the sum did not reach more than a few dozen infected.

"Does everyone actually need to go home?" was the question that Ciasca and others asked themselves almost every day that month.

– They don't, – replied Marco, after consulting with the other executives.

The exception in the Americas was Gladis Orsi, vice president of business development stationed in the United States. After all, unlike the rest of the continent, deaths were registered in the country – 18 people by March 6. In the coming weeks, Gladis would be startled by the evolution of the pandemic, not only there but also in the Philippines, which was home to Stefanini's delivery center that served American customers.

Finally, on March 11, the World Health Organization (WHO) classified the outbreak as a pandemic. The next day, Kothe learned that the government of Romania had declared a state of emergency. Rigorous measures were soon likely to be implemented, even without any deaths yet reported – the first in the country would only happen on March 23. The reason for these drastic measures – even without fatalities – was the fact that Romania is one of the poorest countries in Europe. The government feared it would not be able to deal with a very intense demand in the health sector. That same day, Marco arrived in Mexico with Graça, still believing that life would go on as usual. From there, they planned to continue their trip to the United States, expecting to return to Brazil only at the end of the month.

In the following days, the virus spread across the world at a frightening pace. Dozens of countries in Asia, Africa, and Latin America – which had cases up until that point – reported their first infections. By mid-March, it was starting to become difficult to pinpoint a country on the map that had not yet been touched by SARS-CoV-2.

That week, with Marco and Graça still in Mexico, Stefanini's board held a virtual meeting. "We're going to have to go home," said Stefanini's founder. It was a gigantic challenge: 25,000 employees worldwide would have to work remotely. To complicate matters further, a small part of them were still in-company, assigned to the client's facilities. And everyone, inside or outside the client, could face the problem of the lack of adequate infrastructure at home, be it a stable internet connection or a computer with enough configuration to run the necessary systems and applications.

Internally, Stefanini would need to make adjustments to its equipment and systems, which could further delay the office shutdown process. The experience of 150 people working from home until 2021 did not help face the challenges that lay ahead. Not everyone had a laptop, some still used desktop computers. There wasn't enough material to supply all the employees, and work couldn't stop.

Despite the challenges, the decision had been made. An emergency committee was created, virtually bringing together the leaders of each region. That week, Stefanini would have to be turned upside down. They immediately decided to send home everyone who was considered to be at high risk for COVID-19. It was Monday, March 16, 2020, and the next day employees in this group were supposed to stay home.

In that moment of uncertainty and panic, Marco reacted as he always did during crises: he reinforced communication with employees as much as possible. In moments of insecurity, he felt it was essential to offer information. This repeated what he had done in other crises, such as that of 2008-2009, when he wrote emails to all employees to remind them that, for Stefanini, "a crisis is synonymous with opportunity."

This time, the message would be different. Everyone was quite familiar with what constituted Stefanini's culture. For that previous crisis, Marco also spoke about controlling costs and being aware of opportunities. This time, his emphasis would be different. Mainly because the fear was greater. Many companies suffered from being forced to interrupt their operations and even close their doors. The fears included putting one's life at risk by the virus and losing one's job. However, in this regard, Stefanini could say something that mattered.

Now, instead of writing an email, Marco sent word that he would hold a conference call. All Stefanini employees were invited. The chat was scheduled for Tuesday, March 17th. The initiative became known as the "Town Hall." In that first conversation, still amidst the confusion and chaos in the world, Marco focused on security and stability. There were no layoffs in sight, and Stefanini would be required more than ever by its clients, who needed to maintain operations even during this trying time. By opting for a policy of communication and transparency, the goal was to transmit security so that employees could move on to the next stages in the midst of the pandemic.

The next day, Marco convened the CEOs to assess the situation in each region. In Europe, which bore the brunt of the crisis thus far – with the Italian catastrophe threatening to spread to other countries – there was the greatest immediate risk for Stefanini. After the state of emergency, which had already been decreed, more drastic measures would come, and the population was already attempting to stock up on food. That same day, Belgium, where Tania was, went into lockdown. Over the next few weeks, she would be stopped three times in the street by the police as she went out to buy groceries. Each citizen had two hours to leave and return home.

Marco knew that the European operations depended on three countries: Romania, Poland, and Moldova. That was where Stefanini's delivery centers for the region were located. If an absolute lockdown were enacted in these places, access to offices would be difficult, even when it came to shipping equipment, and customers would be left without their service.

– How are you guys doing, Farlei? – Marco asked the Rio Grande do Sul native about the situation in EMEA, already fearing the answer.

– Bah, I already have half of my people at home! – Kothe replied triumphantly.

In fact, he was being modest. Around 65% of his employees already worked from home. Each week, he had been testing 20% more. By that weekend, the total would reach 85% of the entire team. On Saturday, the 21st, the Romanian government would tighten its grip, with a curfew starting at 10 pm, closing shopping malls and placing a ban on groups of more than three people on the streets. But the European operation was saved. The entire delivery migrated to a work-from-home approach, without any interruption or change in quality, thanks to the gradual and planned process that Kothe had been carrying out for months. While all of Europe was being hit by the first wave of COVID-19, Stefanini already had its structure in place, with its employees at home and ready to serve customers.

As the EMEA region transitioned smoothly, attention turned to the rest of the branches, with offices being emptied out of the blue. In addition to technical issues, there were unexpected details, such as ergonomics. In many places, it was necessary to go to the office to obtain chairs suitable for remote work. It was issues like these that the planned transition in Europe was able to anticipate. Now, the challenge was to replicate this process in the rest of the world.

CHAPTER 18

EVERYWHERE

The story continued as Spencer Gracias, CEO for Stefanini in the North America and Asia Pacific regions, shared his experience with Marco. He explained that employees from Stefanini's Philippines operation had converted an entire floor of the building into housing, and they decided to sleep in the office. The Philippines branch was crucial for Stefanini as English is one of the official languages in the country, making it a common base to serve companies worldwide, particularly in the United States. If the operation in the Philippines were to be interrupted, numerous clients in several countries would be left without service.

The decision to sleep in the office came about because the Philippine government had declared a state of public calamity, leading to disruptions in public transportation in Manila, the capital region. Faced with this situation, the employees had a dilemma: if they went back home, they would not be able to return to work. After a brief meeting, the Filipino team chose to stay and sleep at their workplace. The following day, without any guidance from management, some employees who lived nearby rushed home, prepared food, and brought it back to those who couldn't go home.

This story surprised Stefanini's management, as they had not anticipated such dedication and commitment from their employees. Meanwhile, the global vice president of People and Culture at Stefanini, Rodrigo Pádua, contacted Graça (Marco's partner) out of concern for two other employees who might be stranded away from home. Pádua advised Graça to take Marco, put him on a plane, and return to Brazil immediately.

Although Marco still insisted on sticking to their plan of going to the United States to handle the crisis there, Graça recognized the risk and demanded that they return to Brazil as soon as possible. Her intuition proved correct because the next day, the United States suspended flights to both Mexico and Brazil.

On March 16, Marco and Graça arrived in Brazil and stayed in São Paulo for four days before going to their home in Jaguariúna. From there, Marco coordinated the technology staff to ensure that everyone could work from home. Overcoming this initial phase, they faced the second obstacle: many employees lacked optimal internet connections. The day-to-day challenges were similar to those encountered by the team in Europe.

The Stefanini Europe experience was useful and served as a reference. During the office-to-home migration process, Stefanini was aware of potential problems and how to solve them. Procedures were developed to quickly implement VPNs and adjust internet connections and the work environment – from the computer to the office furniture – so that the employee would have the same tools and comfort as in a traditional office. Thus, in a few days and in a methodical manner, the transition was made without disrupting services. On March 22nd, the majority of Stefanini employees worldwide – 25,000 people in 41 countries – were already working from home.

The last of the executives to leave Stefanini in São Paulo was vice-president Rodrigo Pádua. When he left the office, 90% of the company was already home. The 10% that remained were those who supported essential services, such as call center employees who served hospitals, the emergency hotline, and other services that could not stop, in addition to some clients

225

who did not accept to be served by remote workers. When other countries started to undergo lockdowns, Stefanini teams were able to use the experience they had gained recently and became task forces to help clients make the same move.

For many employees, the experience separated them from friends and neighbors. While some took the opportunity to take a vacation or rest, stuck at home feeling bored, Stefanini teams around the world worked around the clock. It was like being part of a war effort, helping the world so it wouldn't stop, even in the face of that catastrophe. This was Tania's experience in Brussels, for instance. Her husband worked as a real estate agent and could not visit apartments or houses, being forced to stay in his house, with nothing to do. Meanwhile, Tania frantically communicated with clients and employees in different countries.

At that time, the expectation was that the confinement would last only a few weeks. As we know, that wasn't the case. Although the most severe lockdown, carried out in some countries, became more flexible according to the flow of virus variants, the situation would not get back to normal anytime soon. Social distancing was going to last much longer than they could have anticipated, and the new way of working was here to stay.

But the reaction was different in each country. The day after Stefanini managed to get everyone working remotely, many still underestimated the seriousness of covid-19. In Brazil, a full lockdown was never actually carried out, and the pandemic was never truly brought under control, which allowed the virus to spread through the population almost freely – unlike in several other countries, which were much more successful in containing covid-19. At Stefanini, the stance adopted was one of total support for sanitary measures. Marco himself would spend most of his time working in Jaguariúna until 2021. He would only resume international trips after taking the first dose of the vaccine.

On social media, Stefanini's founder publicly took a stand against mass layoffs. If entrepreneurs reacted with fear, closing their doors and leaving employees without jobs, the economic crisis could take on catastrophic proportions. With the weight of a Brazilian multinational, which in 2019 had earned BRL 3.3 billion, he would become in the following months one of the main Brazilian leaders of the #nãodemita (#do not fire) movement.

A new conversation with all employees, the "Town Hall", was held on March 24th. The purpose was to show that they were ready, that the transition was working, sharing incredible cases like the one in the Philippines, highlighting the value of those employees. Marco called them unsung heroes. Stefanini hadn't stopped.

Each day, the CEOs discovered how employees solved problems for a client or for Stefanini itself. Information was shared in Marco's daily meetings with regional CEOs, showing that cells were not waiting for guidance to come from above in order to act. From interns to the CEOs, the reports then became part of the "Town Hall" with the employees when the story of each "unsung hero" was told.

This was the aspect of the crisis that better illustrated Stefanini's identity. There was no single leader providing a recipe of what should be done so that everyone could follow it without questioning or making mistakes. On the contrary, instead of waiting for an order from some central command to make decisions, each leader sought to rely heavily on their own initiative. And each member of the teams understood that the key was to make the process work in their regions with minimal impact. Based on this spirit, strongly rooted in the company's culture, individual work ensured that the entire company would continue to operate normally around the world, even with all those changes.

This feat surprised the clients, who were scared to make such a radical and sudden transition. In the days that followed, CEOs began to receive emails from executives who were impressed that their service had not been disrupted. A London-based Italian-American manufacturing executive wrote, "I must say that your commitment in this extraordinary situation is off the charts." Another message came from one of the best-known global consumer brands: "Your hard work, dedication, and enthusiasm did not go unnoticed."

The executive of a British bank posted his appreciation on his social media pages, saying that they would not have been able to go through that period, when employees were not used to working from home, without Stefanini's help. A German company reported that those two weeks of adaptation had been "painful", but that the support had been "exceptional" and they had "managed to overcome it together." Along the same lines, a Swiss engineering company reported that during that period, the demand for tech customer service had increased by 30%. And, even with this growth and the difficulties of the pandemic, Stefanini managed to satisfy its users. The executive even listed several words of gratitude he had received from his employees.

The list was endless, in a quantity and warmth none of the executives had ever received before. It's not unusual to be thanked, but those messages were effusive. One of the customers thanked them "from the bottom of his heart." In mid-April, a new Town Hall was held, this time telling employees about the feedback they were getting from clients. The message was that the effort had been noticed and recognized for its worth.

In retrospect, one could posit that there was only one explanation for the success at such an intense level in such an extremely adverse scenario: the culture that Stefanini had managed to disseminate among its employees. If they worked under a centralized organization in Brazil, waiting for orders to come from above, it is almost certain that it would not have worked. Days or even weeks would have passed, with services disrupted in various parts of the world.

In contrast, every employee in every cell used the autonomy, empowerment, and trust that had been disseminated for years. This was also the result of the seven attitudes that Graça defended as fundamental and that she summed up with her phrase "liking people." Thanks to this set of qualities that defined Stefanini's identity, the service was never disrupted and the quality was praised more than ever.

However, Stefanini could not be content with the praise of clients, who were enthusiastic about being served in a time of crisis. If that situation was going to last – with the gains that the remote model brought – then it was necessary to implement metrics to ensure constant service quality.

The man for the task was Rodrigo Pádua, Stefanini's global vice president of People and Culture. He had arrived at the company exactly one year prior, in April 2019. He had experience at Ambev, Gafisa, and Danone, and in the latter, he had precisely created its performance gauges – the KPIs, Key Performance Indicators. An innovative project because although the KPIs were often discussed, their implementation was rarely successful. Companies used to struggle to use the collected information to have a true impact on their corporate culture. Pádua arrived at Stefanini willing to implement and use the indicators effectively, while supervising and helping to

229

consolidate the ongoing process of bringing the company's culture to all continents.

Pádua's challenges included monitoring and adjusting the implementation of remote work, a task that became crucial during the pandemic. The expectation was that the construction of culture in that new model would take at least two years. This was just so that it could be developed, with the creation of pilots, with the proper evaluations and corrections. Consolidation in all branches, reaching optimal levels in the indicators, would surely take much longer. The situation was even worse in Brazil. While some pilot projects in other countries showed good indicators, the Brazilian operation lagged behind in terms of remote work. Everything indicated that the process would take many years to be corrected.

With the pandemic, the entire process became spectacularly compressed. Two years' work was carried out in two days, causing offices to be closed overnight and people to work from home the next day. A consolidation that could take between three and five years to be implemented globally – even according to some moderates – had to be completed in fifteen days.

Now was the critical time for Padua, when he would have to test the effectiveness of Stefanini's new way of working. With 90% of all global employees deployed remotely and with no secure prospect of coming back, he began to keep an eye on three metrics: productivity, customer satisfaction, and employee engagement. In the case of engagement, the measurement was made through quick daily surveys sent out to groups of people. Padua was encouraged by the first results. He expected to find serious problems to be corrected, but the result surprised him. "Looks like this remote model isn't so bad; in fact, it seems pretty good," he thought.

Even so, caution prevailed. One concern was that government incentives granted to companies to weather the crisis could be distorting their good performance. When the incentives ended, there was a surprise: the indicators were still positive, even in Brazil.

One of the indicators that most surprised Padua was the one they call the "promoter score," which measures client satisfaction. The survey proved what the praise at the most critical period had indicated: clients were still satisfied. On the side of the employees, this was also true. Usually done annually, Padua decided to divide the survey into smaller questionnaires to be applied more consistently during the pandemic. Another positive surprise. All indicators pointed upwards, with steady improvement. The later return to normality, already in 2022, did not change the results.

Another concern of the executive was that the commitment of the employees would decrease when the adrenaline of the crisis disappeared and the novelty of working at home became routine. "Will the performance and discipline be maintained, or was the initial enthusiasm responsible for all that success?" Padua thought.

Again, surveys measuring engagement showed that the positive attitude was sustained. At the same time, productivity increased by 10%. Looking at the whole, Padua came to the conclusion that the changes to Stefanini would be permanent. Not the excitement of the heat of the crisis, but the result of an evolution and trends that had already been taking place and were now consolidating. A part of the workforce could even go back to the office, but the possibility of working from home was here to stay.

So much so that in May 2020, the project "Stefanini Everywhere" was announced in Brazil. The proposal was to identify talent anywhere in the country, in a world where it was possible to work from anywhere. In addition to Stefanini's own experience, the idea was based on research such as that of Fundação Dom Cabral and Talenses, which consulted 375 companies in Brazil. Over 70% of them confirmed their intention of adopting a partial or full-time remote work modality after the pandemic. In the industry, the index was even higher, with 80% indicating a preference for the new model. In the area of services, remote work would completely dominate the scenario, with 89% of companies seduced by the advantages of working from home. Only trade, due to the need for direct contact with customers, still expected resistance to that evolution.

Certain that this was the way forward, Padua made preparations to ensure that everywhere would work. It wasn't enough to count on the momentary acceptance of employees and a decent technological infrastructure. If Stefanini did not maintain ties with employees in their homes, which is the relationship that ensures the company's corporate identity, the model would not be sustainable, and good performance could deteriorate over time. It was necessary to pay attention to these sociocultural aspects.

The solution was to insist, even after the climax of the crisis, on what Marco considered fundamental: constant communication. More than ever, leaders and employees needed to keep talking. Therefore, Marco and the CEO committee made the decision to maintain the Town Hall. In September 2020, they made the last one entirely dedicated to the topic of the pandemic, but they continued to periodically have conversations with employees addressing various topics.

In addition to the Town Hall, Padua intensified the frequency of employee surveys. In other ways, communication should be a two-way street, conveying to employees the news they received from the front, what was being planned, and what was wanted from them. But, at the same time, paying attention to how they felt and what they wanted.

Padua quickly found that employees were happy working from home. The fear of losing their jobs had been replaced by a desire for the Everywhere model to continue. In part, because the pandemic was still raging. But not just that. They were comfortable, they had more time, and their quality of life had improved. Staying at home was better.

Not for everyone and not necessarily all the time. In surveys, about 40% of people wanted to work at the office, even if they were comfortable working from home. Some indicated their preference for a hybrid model, alternately working at the office and from home.

Based on the surveys, Padua realized that many people missed meeting their colleagues, and that not having the obligation to follow the strict office schedule from Monday to Friday worked well for certain profiles. Others found that they lacked the ideal conditions to work at home, either because of the presence of children or pets, or because they had a partner who works in the same environment, or even because of the lack of their own separate space to use as an office. These profiles preferred to return to the conventional space.

From Padua's perspective, all models could be used. Once the worst period of the pandemic had passed, there was no longer a need to keep 100% of people at home. Everywhere could work if it adopted an inclusive, flexible, hybrid format. During the worst moment of the pandemic, even call centers worked from home, although these cases were in the minority. What mattered was whether the arrangement was good for the client, for the employee, and for Stefanini.

Gradually, the ideal percentage of employees at home was adjusted. At its peak in 2020, remote work reached 95%. With the drop in COVID cases in the second half of the following year, the proportion became more balanced. Some started going to the office once or twice a week.

It was through experience and research that Padua and the other CEOs discovered that there is no ideal ratio. They have to be flexible and adaptable according to the moment, the employee's profile, and the client's needs. Stefanini started to offer different possibilities, such as working from home 100% of the time or alternating with two or three days at home. For those who live too far from the base, an arrangement was offered for working a few weeks at the office and the rest of the year at home.

With the implementation of flexible work policies, Padua started receiving stories of employees who were leaving the cities where they previously worked in-person. Instead, they were choosing places that suited them better and where they could save on housing expenses. Even Padua's own team now had employees living in different countries such as Canada, Portugal, and others.

This reminded Padua of his own youth when he had to leave his hometown of Lavras, a town in Minas Gerais, 240 kilometers away from Belo Horizonte, in search of job opportunities. Today, a young person from Lavras could compete on an equal footing with a young person from São Paulo, New York, or Berlin. Before the pandemic, Stefanini had employees in 1,600 cities worldwide, but the company was commonly associated with having only 77 offices. However, in 2021, the company would end the year with employees in 2,688 cities. This was not just a quantitative leap but also a shift in how the company accounted for its staff.

Now, the company was no longer restricted to hiring people who lived in cities where Stefanini already had a presence. New hires could come from anywhere. The focus shifted from physical location to what truly mattered: dedication, relevant knowledge, and capacity. What was once a utopian dream, the concept of Stefanini Everywhere, had become a reality.

CHAPTER 19

THE CHILD OF CRISIS

T he emails were no longer answered, phones rang and no one answered. At the end of February 2022, the nearly 50 employees in Ukraine who served Stefanini clients disappeared. In desperation, Tania Herrezeel in Brussels and Farlei Kothe in Romania exchanged messages, trying to imagine what could have happened. Part of the fear came from what they had read in the press. In the early hours of February 24, shortly after midnight, Russian troops entered Ukraine from the border with Belarus. Shortly thereafter came the tanks. In the following hours, there were reports of missiles exploding in different parts of the territory, including the Ukrainian capital, Kiev. The news quickly traveled to Brussels and Bucharest, where Tania and Kothe were respectively located. The lack of information about the Ukraine-based team made everyone terribly restless.

For the first time since World War II, the European continent witnessed the invasion of one sovereign territory by another, generating a full-scale military conflict between both countries. Based on evidence that the Ukrainian office was indeed empty, Kothe, Tania, and the other executives engaged every contact they had. Clients were served by the local Kiev-based team through a Ukrainian partner company, yet Kothe and his colleagues in Bucharest felt responsible for them. They needed to understand what was happening and where those professionals were.

What little contact they managed was limited to WhatsApp messages, as conventional communications had stopped working. They learned that some professionals, out of fear, tried to leave the capital, but the exits were blocked; both on the roads and in the airspace, which was closed. Trains leaving the city were crowded. Those who managed to get close to one of the borders by car, such as with Romania, Moldova, or Poland, had to abandon their vehicles on crowded roads and walk for dozens of kilometers, with all their family members, including children, in tow. The government even banned men aged between 18 and 60 from leaving the country, as they had to join the defense forces against the invader.

In Romania, Kothe felt powerless. Stefanini's local partner in Ukraine was trying to help, but nobody knew how to react. With the obstacles to leaving and the government ban, many went in search of shelter, a task that in some cases would take days. They discovered that some members of the team had gone to serve in the Army, fighting on the front lines. Others sought to protect themselves from bombing and were located in bunkers, both official, provided by the government, and improvised ones, such as underground subway stations. Concerned, Kothe wanted to know if they could be removed from the country. Some were prevented, summoned by the Army, others simply chose to stay. There was nothing left to do.

The sentiment was one of shock and bewilderment all around. The planet had not even recovered from the previous collapse, the pandemic, and a new crisis was emerging to terrorize humanity. At the beginning of 2022, the technology sector could at least be proud of having played a crucial role in keeping the world running. Instead of a forced interruption, the IT segment – alongside the health sector – was the one that worked the hardest. And among major companies, few were as active as Stefanini. In spite of the crisis, the overall assessment was definitely positive in the period: between 2017 and 2022, Ebitda was multiplied by four. The recovery of the years 2015-2016 – when it did not shrink, but did not grow either – was consolidated. After growing 7% in 2017 and 2018, it rose to 10.5% in 2019 and then – precisely during the crisis – it soared. The company grew 20% in 2020 and an incredible 25% in 2021. All expectations were that this pace would continue.

None of that was achieved through budget cuts or layoffs. While the rest of the market became desperate and the competition carried out massive layoffs, at Stefanini the number rose continuously, from 24,000 employees in 2018 to 30,000 in 2022. This expansion was carried out completely remotely, thanks to the Everywhere model. From the admission process and selection and hiring procedures to training and mentoring, everything was done end-to-end, without the need for the candidate to be physically present in the offices.

Upon entering the new Stefanini, adapted to operate in a different world, the employee encountered a reality that was very different from before 2022. Everywhere – from Kiev to São Paulo, from Montevideo to Manila – the market had become digital. Customs have changed; even trade fairs ceased to exist, at least temporarily. The reinvention reached the forms of communication at corporate and personal levels. Employees could no longer go to the office, company events, or the supermarket. The trends, which were accelerated by the pandemic, were here to stay, and Stefanini was at the forefront of this trend.

Not without a lot of work, tests, and measurements. It took two years of fine-tuning, seeking the best of both worlds – virtual and in-person –, combining the flexibility of working from home with face-to-face rituals that allowed for integration and learning among employees. Within this period, the number of offices was inevitably reduced. Some were closed, others migrated to the co-working model. In some cities, entire floors were returned, even as thousands of employees were admitted between the start and end of the pandemic. Those that continued to exist changed their appearance, with fewer family photos and more "plug and play" tables, where the employee finds an available table, works, interacts, holds meetings, and is back at home the next day. Physical areas could also be reduced, with a decrease in the flow of employees. It was no longer possible to backpedal on the remote model: everyone could no longer fit the office space.

Paradoxically, the number of locations with company offices increased: now there were 2,500 cities, 720 of which in Brazil. After all, Everywhere allowed talent to be located anywhere, with flexibility, savings, and ensuring the company's digital transformation. At the same time, Stefanini's position in the world was reaffirmed. According to a 2021 study by Fundação Dom Cabral, Stefanini was the fifth most internationalized company in Brazil, considering assets, revenues, and employees abroad. It was the fourth in terms of assets, the seventh in revenues, and the sixth in the number of employees, in the relation between these items abroad and the company's total assets. With a presence in 41 countries, it is also the one with the most subsidiaries owned around the world among national businesses.

Given the figures, which are surprising considering such an overwhelming crisis, there was only one possible conclusion: Stefanini's culture – based on personal responsibility and resilience – had protected the company. Better yet, there was a leap in terms of management, making customers and employees impressed – in some cases even proud – with the way they had faced the biggest crisis of the last decades.

All this work of transmitting and managing this DNA has been transferred, to a great extent, to the virtual realm. The weekly conference held with all employees during the pandemic – each CEO speaking to their region, with Marco by their side – was maintained, being transformed into a monthly event. At first, the specific subject was COVID-19 and the measures being taken, and later it began to include other relevant topics, which were relayed to employees. Likewise, the first crisis committee, which brought together all the CEOs in the world, continued to be held every Tuesday.

Gradually, they realized that the way people related to each other was changing. "The online model unites those who are far away and distances those who are closer," summarized Rodrigo Pádua, the man who is always on the lookout for trends. In a way, Stefanini, being geographically dispersed, had the best results with digitization – unlike couples that cannot stop using WhatsApp while they are together. The numerous virtual conversations between CEOs, managers, and teams brought people closer together. Employees got used to hearing their CEOs speak, each in their region. In North America and Asia Pacific, Spencer Gracias; in Europe, Middle East, and Africa, Farlei Kothe; in Latin America, Damian Mendez; in Brazil, Marcelo Ciasca. And the CEOs, in turn, met a lot more people than before; they saw their children, their dogs, and even a little bit of their homes.

It was in this environment, both close and distant, that the absence of the Ukrainian employees was felt. Connected from other countries, Stefanini employees were forced to imagine that the friendly face, which said "hello" on the computer screen, had put on a uniform and left for the battlefront. Either that or they were in a bunker, afraid a missile would fall at any moment.

A week after the start of the invasion of Ukraine, information circulated in the press that another country could be the target of military aggression. It was Moldova, a country of 2.6 million inhabitants, located between Ukraine and Romania. Like the previously invaded country, Moldova also had a region disputed with Russia – Transnistria –, thus creating the possibility that the conflict would extend to it. If that happened, a large part of customer service in the entire region covered by Farlei – Europe, Middle East, and Africa – could be disrupted. Stefanini had an important branch there, with 250 employees, located in the capital, Chisinau.

"I need to get them out of there," said Farlei.

Kothe knew that the cost would be high and that it would come out of his own budget, reducing his Ebitda, the criterion by which he himself was remunerated. That didn't matter. The important thing was to get those people out of there. He called the team, and together, they defined what had to be done. They arranged transport for anyone wanting to leave Moldova for Romania and then began to discuss where they would stay. The mass of refugees leaving Ukraine had already reduced the number of available accommodations in Bucharest. They listed places where those displaced could stay: in addition to hotels and Airbnb, even some Romanian employees offered to accommodate some people.

In a few hours, the plan was ready. With this information in hand, Kothe called Brazil, where he managed to speak with Marco and Graça. Without mentioning the cost issue to them, he quickly presented the situation, still not knowing exactly how many people would come. Even in Ukraine, with missiles falling and tanks moving, many chose not to leave the country. Kothe estimated that he could welcome something like 50 or 60 people each week.

"We'll back whatever you say," Marco replied.

The next day, they proceeded to carry out the plan. To avoid disruptions in services and also to give people time to organize themselves, the plan was to carry out the transfers during the weekends. They got in touch with the branch and advised: whoever had their documentation up to date and so wished could inform their name and that of their party. The response was immediate. On Sunday, February 27, 2022, the first group of Moldovans arrived in Bucharest, 27 employees and their families, totaling 52 people.

The following Saturday, March 6th, a new group arrived in Bucharest, this time with 66 people. So Kothe suggested a Town Hall in the company office with the entire Moldovan team. It was the meeting that the executive committee of the European team held every day, usually first thing in the morning.

Three days later, they all met at the Stefanini office. It was a Wednesday, at lunchtime, but even so, the building was mostly empty. Kothe went up to the third floor, which was completely dark, except for one room, where the local team and the Moldovans were waiting. The meeting was expected to last thirty minutes, during which he would deal with matters relating to both teams, Ukraine and Moldova, including details of the transfer, internal and client communication, and definition of the next actions. He had also thought of a positive and supportive message to say in front of them, but he was unprepared for the scene he found.

In the room, there were dozens of families, most of them with small children, who had left behind their homes, belongings, and even loved ones, who could not or did not want to leave. Kothe recognized some of the faces, whom he had never met in person but were closer now than when they spoke online. Despite the large group, there was relative silence.

Still a little uneasy, he started to give his prepared message when he suddenly lost his voice. A girl, four or five years old, drew a picture in front of him. She reminded him of his daughter, who was the same age. He felt weak. The same thing could happen to him and his family.

He ended his message, knowing that he would never forget that scene. He also wished that no one he knew, colleagues, or family, had to go through that.

The following Saturday, March 13th, a third group arrived in Bucharest. In total, adding the three of them, more than 170 people, including employees, family members, and anyone else they wished to take, left Moldova and were taken to Romania by Stefanini. Psychological support was offered to each family, and all the necessary documentation was provided so that they could stay.

After some time, the situation became stable. Ukraine was resisting the invasion, and it was clear that, at least in the short term, Russia would not be able to create another hotbed of conflict. Feeling safer, some refugee employees decided they could return to Moldova. A short time later, much to Kothe's frustration, the Romanian government also requested that they leave, as their home country was not at war. Everyone went back, now knowing that, in case of an emergency, Stefanini would always be ready to help.

Some time after the employees were welcomed, Marco warned Kothe that the expense would not be billed to the European operation. The head offices would pay for it all. This concern for employees was an example of how connected the entire world was now. Stefanini needed to face these changes inside and outside the company. After all, connectivity has not only changed the relationships between people within companies. As pointed out by Executive Vice President Ailtom

Nascimento, the pandemic accelerated the upcoming wave throughout the market. The connectivity that has transformed customs and ways of working has also changed other interactions within retail, education, government, and financial services. "Consumers were the main driver in the changes enacted by digital transformation," observed Nascimento.

The immediate result was an increase in the demand for digital solutions, such as for retail. What was a trend became a present reality, and companies became more interested in cloud computing, digital marketing, and cybersecurity. At the same time, every resource that allowed for productivity increases also advanced, such as Agile Development, a methodology for developing and testing new solutions.

Now, topics approached by futurology were at hand and became part of companies' plans. Some are already looking into instant purchases, where consumers buy products in the middle of a game or TV show they are watching on a streaming service, pausing the scene and tapping on the item being shown. Others are preparing to serve loyal customers in a personalized way, with a system that alerts the company when the customer has entered the store to offer them something they usually purchase.

All of this will require a high level of integration between systems, including the use of artificial intelligence to help manage each logistical component, while preserving sustainability and real-time inventories. It's like a game of dominoes, where one more sophisticated feature requires perfecting the next. For this reason, companies are also investing increasingly more in the concept of resilience in the supply chain, which permeates all lines of activity, such as health, technology, education, and industry. In turn, this will be boosted with the arrival of 5G and with machine-to-machine interactions, accelerating the entire delivery service, customer service, production, etc. More connectivity will reinforce the process that brings the future into the present.

In order to meet the current demand and organize itself for the future, Stefanini prepared itself to continue pursuing acquisitions, adding more and more value to services. Right at the start of the pandemic crisis, the search for opportunities had been suspended, given the uncertainty in the market.

"Will there be enough money?" an employee asked.

"Will our clients continue to pay?" said another.

But in a couple of months, in May 2020, an executive decided to raise the issue of acquisitions again: the Vice President of People and Culture, Rodrigo Pádua, a newcomer who had not even completed a year on the job. The questioning took place at one of the emergency meetings of the CEOs, held every Tuesday. There, Pádua mentioned that the signs were positive, with no cash problems in sight, and clients paying on time. It was time to put the pedal to the metal, not to brake.

If acquiring companies in normal times is already a sign of health, in times of crisis there are even more opportunities for better purchases. "There are three types of companies in a crisis", analyzes Pádua. "The ones that are left behind; those that take too long to make decisions, stall and need an extensive recovery; and those that make a decision and accelerate." Stefanini was among the latter.

In total, during the pandemic, ten companies were acquired. Most, as previously discussed, were from the financial and digital areas, with the leadership of Jorge Iglesias, at Topaz, and Guilherme Stefanini, at the Haus group. But others would also arrive, like the Peruvian Sapia, with its software as a service and a portfolio of 180 clients. Or Acsa, a company that manufactures electrical panels and structures for electrical centers, used by companies in different industries.

In general, the acquisitions were 100% linked to the accelerated digital transformation process. If the change were organic, it would take much longer. In the digital age, the speed of the pandemic dictated the pace. So much so that some of them were managed remotely for over a year, even though they were larger companies than Stefanini's previous standard, bringing 400 or even 700 employees into the group. Only in 2022 were they visited in person by the board.

The acquisitions once again confirmed Stefanini's profile and path: investing in the midst of crises, operating through several companies, being digital and adding value towards the future. Simultaneously speaking to two worlds, technology and business. On the one hand, exploring the traditional relationship with CIOs; in the other, talking to bank chairpersons, product executives, marketing vice presidents. The multiplicity of dialogue channels is another aspect that has made Stefanini into a flexible, diverse and resilient business.

However, these characteristics, currently present in Stefanini's culture, also need to be perpetuated in the next generation of executives. Such as among Marco's children, the executives Guilherme and Rodrigo Stefanini. The former is already looking to the future, leading Haus, the group's digital marketing platform. The latter, Rodrigo, took over as country manager in Chile in 2021. Before that, he had started his career focusing on strategy and digital transformation. He worked at Somos Educação, at the consulting firm Bain & Company and at the investment manager XP Inc.

From his experience, Rodrigo witnessed the importance of flexibility, of learning and reacting quickly when necessary. Even though they took different paths, he arrived at conclusions very similar to those of his father. As it is not possible to predict what the market will be like in the future, he defined his personal identity as that of a constant learner. "Five years from now, everything will have changed", he imagines, having turned 27 in 2022. "We don't know what it will be, but it will change."

The profile of the new generation seems adequate when considering the challenges that Stefanini may face. Because only one is for certain: new crises will come. The recent period of instability, one of the most difficult in the history of global capitalism, will not be the last. Others will occur, either through economic collapses or in the form of major technological or behavioral changes. With all the uncertainties, the only constant that contemporary society offers is the guarantee of change.

Even so, that company that started from nothing in a small room on Avenida Paulista will be in a unique position – with its peculiar culture of autonomy and agility – to adapt, grow and serve its clients. Because it is the company that was born, developed, and prospered in the hardest of times. Stefanini and its culture are the children of crisis.